John Muir:

A Naturalist in Southern California

Eaton Canyon Falls, Pasadena, soon after they were first seen by John Muir in 1877. *[Courtesy of the Archives of the Pasadena Historical Museum]*

JOHN MUIR
A Naturalist in Southern California

Elizabeth Pomeroy

MANY
MOONS
PRESS

© 2001 by Elizabeth Pomeroy

John Muir: A Naturalist in Southern California was produced by Regina Books and printed by Cushing-Malloy, Inc.

Book design by Mark Morrall Dodge.

Cover design and art direction by Hortensia Chu. She also created the Many Moons Press logo.

Pen and ink illustrations by Joseph Stoddard.

ISBN 0-9700481-1-4

Cover photographs:
   Front cover: Muir in the Pasadena home of T.P. Lukens,
      about 1896
   Back cover: Muir in the Southern California desert

MANY
MOONS
PRESS

P.O. Box 94505
Pasadena, California 91109

PRINTED IN THE UNITED STATES OF AMERICA

For John W. Robinson,
historian, hiker, teacher and friend

Contents

Acknowledgments   9

Chapter 1: Orange Groves and Elfin Forest

 1870s & 1880s: Earliest Southern California visits and
 mountain explorations; Congers and Carrs; keeping in
 touch; domestic commitments   13

Chapter 2: Trees, Friends, and Letters Thick as
 Snowflakes

 1890s: Meeting new friends; conservation alliances;
 kindred spirits and contrasting styles:
 Lukens and Lummis   29

Chapter 3:   Mountain Riches in Public Life

 1900s & 1910s: Intersecting worlds of science,
 education and politics; forest vigilance; Carnegie and
 Roosevelt; Hooker family, Burroughs, Vroman   51

Chapter 4:   Out Till Sundown

 1910s: Family cares and desert discoveries;
 Sierra Club in Southern California; last words to the
 plants; legacy of names and the spirit   69

Notes on Sources   87

◊

Voices from the Past

 Selections from John Muir's Correspondence
 with T. P. Lukens   93

Selections from John Muir's Correspondence
with Charles Lummis   94

Memories of Camping with John Muir in
Palm Springs, by Helen Lukens Gaut   113

At Dinner with Theodore Roosevelt
in Pasadena   124

Farewell to John Muir, in the *Los Angeles Times*   127

Final Memories of John Muir, in the *Pasadena Star*   136

Places to Visit

Pasadena   143
   Eaton Canyon County Park and Nature Center
   Conger and Carr home sites

Los Angeles   145
   Lummis Home (El Alisal)

The Mountains   145
   Chantry Flat, San Gabriel Mountains
   Chilao Visitor Center, San Gabriel Mountains

The Desert   147
   Daggett
   Indian Canyons, near Palm Springs

Acknowledgments

This is an expanded version of the book *John Muir in Southern California*, printed by the Castle Press of Pasadena in 1999 as a special limited edition. I am grateful to George Kinney for permission to reprint that text.

For encouragement, help, and asking interesting questions, my thanks to Ronald Limbaugh, Peter Wild, Donn Headley, Stanley Hutchinson, Tom Andrews, Steve Mason, Charlie Bell, Hugh Stilley, John Pomeroy and Margaret Pomeroy Hunt, and many Sierra Club friends who always wanted to hear a little more about John Muir. John W. Robinson has been an inspiration to all my historical writings.

I appreciate help from the staffs of the Huntington Library, the Pasadena Historical Museum, the Pasadena Public Library, the Braun Library of the Southwest Museum, and the University Research Library at UCLA. Other libraries and historical societies in Southern California also provided information and leads.

I am grateful to the following for permission to reprint material in their care: the Huntington Library, San Marino, California, for selected letters in the T. P. Lukens Collection; the Southwest Museum, Los Angeles, California, for letters between Charles Lummis and John Muir, MS collection 1.3221; the *Los Angeles Times* for articles commemorating Muir's death in 1914. I appreciate the help of Daryl Morrison of the Holt-Atherton Special Collections at the University of the Pacific, and Ross DeLipkau, Administrator of the Muir-Hanna Trust.

Richard D. Burns and Mark Dodge produced this edition. Hortensia Chu designed the cover and her artistic eye greatly benefitted the book. Six original drawings were created by Joseph Stoddard especially for the book. Warmest thanks to this wonderful team.

ORANGE GROVES AND ELFIN FOREST

Orange Grove Avenue, 1890

✧ *Chapter 1* ✧

Orange Groves and Elfin Forest

IN AUGUST OF 1877, a traveler from San Francisco arrived by sea at Santa Monica. "An hour's ride over stretches of bare, brown plain, and through cornfields and orange groves," he wrote later, "brought me to the handsome, conceited little town of Los Angeles, where one finds Spanish adobes and Yankee shingles meeting and overlapping in very curious antagonism." John Muir was on his way to the village of Pasadena.

Muir was then thirty-nine years old, not yet married, still on his exuberant search for "anyplace that's wild." He had been in California since 1868, when he had walked directly from San Francisco into the Yosemite with its baptism of light, storms and exhilarating climbs. It was friendship that first brought him to Southern California. Back he came in later years for old and new friendships, mountain explorations, and conservation efforts. All formed a continuing thread in his public and private life until that last farewell: his death in Los Angeles in 1914.

On that first visit, Muir found the sunny landscape "checkered with brusque little bits of civilization," but these did not attract him. Instead he turned his sights toward the

San Gabriel Mountains, rising grandly along the northern skyline. He hastened on to the Pasadena Colony, located on the southwest corner of the San Pasqual Rancho. There he would pass a pleasant week of exploring and reminiscing with the family of Dr. O. H. Conger, a friend from his university days in Wisconsin. Other close friends from that time, Ezra and Jeanne Carr, had already bought the property across the road from Conger which would become their "Carmelita" estate, but they had not yet moved to it.

In two letters published later in the *San Francisco Evening Bulletin*, Muir described the scene around him in Pasadena. Muirian metaphors were in full sway. The citrus groves were choice, but the "glorious abundance of ripe sun and soil is only beginning to be coined into fruit." The settlers, he found, "work like ants in a sunny noonday" and "count their orange chickens years or more before they are hatched." But the little colony seemed aristocratic, its conversation "seasoned with a smack of mental ozone, Attic salt."

Curiously, Muir saw no benefit for sick people in the much-praised climate. The spicy fir and pine woods of a Sierra summer would be far more reviving, he believed. High land prices in Pasadena seemed to put the thriving village beyond the reach of poor settlers. But there he found, in 1877, about 60 families of "the better class of vagabond pioneers, who, during their rolling-stone days have managed to gather sufficient gold moss to purchase from 10 to 40 acres of land."

Muir, born in Scotland in 1838, had lived a severe but nature-blessed boyhood on pioneer Wisconsin farmland. In 1861 he went to Madison to enter the University of Wisconsin, an experience that would provide lasting mentors, inspiration for a lifetime of exploring, but no degree. The student population that year was 180. Professor Ezra S. Carr offered classes in chemistry and geology, and Orville H. Conger, eleven years older than Muir, was studying mineralogy there.

In 1863, Muir was restless, lacking funds and pondering the Civil War turmoil coming ever closer. He then departed from Madison for good—just leaving the Wisconsin University for the University of the Wilderness, he said. Thirty years later, articles in the *Pasadena Star* referred to him as "Professor Muir, the glaciologist," a tribute to his self-taught knowledge from the vast outdoor campus he had chosen.

But in his first Southland visit, he was delighted to sojourn at the 30-acre farm of the Congers, located at the southeast corner of Orange Grove Avenue and Colorado Boulevard. Conger had come to Pasadena in 1874 after more than half a lifetime, including medical training and a mining career following his Wisconsin studies. He had discovered the famous Emma Mine in Utah, and is said to have crossed the plains eleven times before the Union Pacific Railroad was built. Like many of the first Pasadena settlers, he was a professional and a gentleman but had little knowledge of orcharding. Yet he and the others were mainly listed as fruit growers in early city directories.

Conger's property occupied a beautiful level table land at the brink of the Arroyo Seco. To the east, a broad expanse of valley sloped downward and away. Across the northern horizon rose the Sierra Madre range, which had summoned John Muir. Citrus and deciduous fruit trees graced the family's property, which was bordered with a rose hedge. A 1000-foot drive from Colorado street led to the frame house and hitching post under pepper trees. On the evening air, the Congers could

O.H. Conger residence in Pasadena, about 1886 *[Courtesy of the Archives at the Pasadena Historical Museum]*

hear the bells of the San Gabriel Mission, three miles to the southeast.

Daughter Lulu Conger, the second child born in Pasadena, recalled that tourists from the East were driven through their grounds, and artists asked to paint their views. Peach trees and an alfalfa patch for the Jersey cow occupied the space where today Rose Parade commentators sit high in television press boxes.

The village center of Pasadena was near to this fruitful spot. In 1886, real estate promoters described the Conger tract as within two minutes walk of the post office, churches, schools, the free public library, and the depot. Mrs. Louise Conger, in fact, had been an organizer and trustee of the library. Later she was a trustee of the Throop Polytechnic Institute (now the California Institute of Technology—Caltech).

The first June "we set out 300 two-year old orange trees west of the house," Mrs. Conger told Hiram Reid for his *History of Pasadena* (1895). "A few months later the grasshoppers came." Undaunted, she and the Doctor covered every tree with muslin and saved them all. Dr. Conger's poem on that horrendous episode shows the high spirits and pioneer pluck of John Muir's friend:

Gloria Tuesday!
Avaunt Grasshoppers!
Ye pestilence that wasteth at noonday!
Dry up, and skedaddle, with your desolating straddle.
Hurry up and jump,
With your slender juicy rump.
Thou omnivorous bold wretch,

Make thy biggest jump and stretch,
While the sands of grace are flowing
Make a hurried hasty going.
Keep a jumping, jumping, jumping,
While our curses are all thumping,
Thumping at thy chamber door,
Fast and hot and evermore,
Cause thou art a bore.

Shades of Dr. Seuss. No wonder Muir treasured his stays in this energetic household. Perhaps he was tempted in 1877 as his friend gestured toward land for sale just beyond his own: "Buy it and be my neighbor," was Dr. Conger's invitation. "Plant five acres with orange trees, and by the time your last mountain is climbed their fruit will be your fortune." Neither friend could guess that a lifetime of mountains lay ahead for John Muir, nor that he would succeed so well with orchards in another place. (His botanizing would be domesticated into fruit ranching, at the Northern California home in Martinez he later shared with his wife and daughters).

During this 1877 visit, Muir also visited groves on the estate of Benjamin D. Wilson and recorded how different species were cultivated. He found plantings of lime, lemon, banana, olive, almond and English walnut in the area, although oranges prevailed. "When a man plants a tree, he plants himself," contemplated Muir. "Every root is an anchor, over which he rests with grateful interest, and becomes sufficiently calm to feel the joy of living...he necessarily makes the acquaintance of the sun and the sky."

Yes, as a visitor, this seemed to John Muir an idyllic life. But his own agricultural years, soon to come, brought no such rest and calm. The sun and sky that *he* knew would always be calling him back to the wild places.

From the Congers' household, Muir set out on his "fine shaggy little five days' excursion" into the San Gabriel Mountains. Mrs. Conger baked three loaves of bread for him and provided tea. This he steeped by putting a little into a bottle of cold water and laying it in the sun. He carried no firearm, unlike most who ventured into the mountain haunts in those days.

Although it seemed gray and unpromising, the range soon surprised him with wild gardens and lilies "big enough for bonnets." Over the following 17 years, Muir wrote about this mountain ramble four times. Each time he polished or rearranged the material, adding different details. Such was his habit as a reluctant author over the rest of his life. The first account of this jaunt was written in a letter to Jeanne Carr (soon to be a Pasadenan herself), with later versions in newspaper and magazine articles. Finally the tale reappeared in the Bee-Pastures chapter of his book *The Mountains of California* (1894).

Muir's route went something as follows: on the first day, in the August heat, he walked as far as the mouth of Eaton Canyon and camped there overnight at the cabin of a solitary water prospector. The next day he reached Eaton Falls and its pool, where he stopped to jot down descriptions of the ferns and mosses in this "charming little poem of wildness." Climbing above the falls, he ascended the west rim of the canyon to the summit now called Muir Peak, then down a flower-filled canyon to present-day Idlehour Trail Camp.

Two more days of exploring found him scrambling, at times creeping, through the bristly elfin forest. "I had to contend with the richest, most self-possessed and uncompromising chaparral I have ever enjoyed since first my mountaineering began," he recalled later. At last he reached a summit, probably a peak just west of Mt. Wilson. From this elevation of about 5,700 feet the landscape spread out as "one vast bee-pasture, a rolling wilderness of honey-bloom."

On the fifth day, already out of bread, he made a quick descent and returned to his hosts. He brought Louise Conger some "tiger lily" bulbs (perhaps they were the Humboldt lilies which still grow grandly to twelve feet in the San Gabriel Mountains). Nineteen years later, Mrs. Conger told historian Hiram Reid that they had blossomed every year since and she always called them her John Muir lilies.

On his way back to San Francisco, Muir wrote in praise of the Southland mountains to another Wisconsin friend soon to settle in Pasadena. This was his devoted confidante Mrs. Jeanne Carr. She had met John Muir in 1860 in Madison, where her husband Dr. Ezra Carr held the University's chair in Natural Science. Both Carrs had served as mentors to Muir in his student days. He always felt they had opened to him "the book of nature," with all the languages, pages and texts he sought to "read" in the natural world. In 1869 Dr. Carr accepted a professorship at Berkeley and he became California's Superintendent of Public Instruction in 1875.

But it was Mrs. Carr, twelve years older than Muir, who corresponded with him during the years he lived in Yosemite, 1868 to 1873. Always she had a ready ear for his perceptions, his theories. To her, as a fellow plant lover, he confided his deep joy in the whole mountain tapestry, from the vast weather to the tiniest alpine gentian. He would later re-affirm these bonds and memories by planting a Sierra sequoia in her Pasadena garden.

With the encouragement of Dr. Conger, the Carrs bought 42 acres of Indiana Colony land in 1877. Soon they would settle directly across Colorado Boulevard from their old Wisconsin friend. Conger had written to them praising the excellent soil, the water supply in living springs, and the intelligent and enterprising community. He personally spaded up and approved some of the land they were considering. For encouragement, he promised to share his water rights if they ever needed more water.

The Carrs paid $75 per acre for their tract, which stretched along Colorado from Orange Grove Avenue to Fair Oaks Avenue. They named their spread Carmelita, meaning "little orchard-garden." It was virgin land except for one edge that had been plowed for hay. Like the Conger property, Carmelita was on the brow of the slope dropping away toward the east, offering fine views.

The Carrs did not become permanent residents until 1880. But the youngest of their four sons, A. L. Carr (Al), "bached" on the property until his parents arrived to build their house. Al, who lived until 1937, wrote some humorous memories of the new estate and also about California adventures with Muir, who had been like one of the family back in Madison days.

For example, Carr tells of this outing in the mid-1870's, when he was about 20 and Muir about 35: "On the termination of a long and arduous trip through the Giant Forest and Kern River Canon with John Muir, I left him at Visalia to continue on South to Los Angeles…the activating motive was to seek forgetfulness of the steady diet of oatmeal to which I had been

Ezra and Jeanne Carr residence at Carmelita, Pasadena, 1886, looking east along Colorado Blvd. Conger residence is at right. [*Courtesy of the Archives at the Pasadena Historical Museum*]

subjected while with John—to which he, as a native Scotchman, was naturally and abnormally addicted—in the aromatic and warming influence of the *chili con carne* and *frijoles con chili* of the langorous South."

Jeanne Carr soon laid out the Carmelita lands in a fruitful blend of order and wildness. She began with pines recalling her Vermont girlhood, then planted a large collection of exotic trees aided by many gifts of seedlings. Coniferous trees of the Pacific Coast grew tall. The orchards contained more than a thousand citrus trees and a thousand other fruit and nut trees. Flower beds and lawns surrounded the house. Instead of fences, she favored hedges—planting Mexican limes along Orange Grove and Pasadena's trademark Cherokee rose twined with grapevines along Colorado. "Plenteous bloom in spring and color for autumn thoughts," she wrote in describing her plans.

Huffing good-naturedly about these artful designs (since he preferred wild nature), Muir nevertheless offered help to his friend. Al Carr remembers that Muir planted at Carmelita both kinds of Sequoia, gigantea and sempervirens, while Sir Joseph Hooker, the curator of London's Kew Botanical Gardens, left for his "calling card" an English yew.

The Carrs built a house at cost of $7,000, substantial then when records show the cost of an average home was about $1,200. But financial difficulty forced the Carrs to sell their house and part of Carmelita in 1892 to Simeon Reed, an Oregon millionaire who later endowed Reed College. The Carrs moved to an adjoining property, but their Pasadena days of visitors and festivities were nearing an end. Ezra Carr died in 1894, and Jeanne Carr, her mind failing, died in San

Francisco's Crocker Home for Old Ladies in 1903. She was never forgotten by John Muir.

Somewhere on the site of the present Norton Simon Museum and its grounds, Dr. Carr had built a Carmelita landmark later described by his son. It was a cabin made of cypress logs to be the Doctor's study and a "sanctuary for the male contingent." The roof was covered by Gold of Ophir roses, the hearth clad in arroyo stones, and the firelight danced on a lifetime's collection of mementos. On the air was the scent of orange blossoms. In this private haven, a rustic outbuilding away from the main house, Carr, Muir, Conger and others could gather.

Such were John Muir's friendships and surroundings in his earliest visits to Southern California. It would be a decade or more before he was a frequent visitor again. Three years

Carr log cabin at Carmelita [*Courtesy of the Archives at the Pasadena Historical Museum*]

after the carefree ramble above Eaton Canyon, Muir married Louie Wanda Strentzel, daughter of Dr. John Strentzel who was a fruit rancher in Martinez, California. Jeanne Carr had introduced them and encouraged the match. Soon Muir was deep into managing part of his father-in-law's 2,600 acres. With daughters Annie Wanda (born 1881) and Helen (born 1886) at hand, the mountaineer's attention settled down upon hearth and orchards. But in time, new friendships—and a dinner party for a U.S. President—would draw him again to the Southland.

STODDARD

El Alisal

✧ *Chapter 2* ✧

Trees, Friends, and Letters
Thick as Snowflakes

THE SAME YEAR that John Muir was married, a future comrade came to settle in Pasadena. Arriving in 1880, Theodore Parker Lukens set out on a path which would later cross Muir's, resulting in a twenty-year bond of friendship. Simply, they were both crazy about trees.

Lukens, who was ten years younger than Muir, was born near New Concord, Ohio, into a Quaker family. His father was in the nursery business and Theodore took up the same work in Rock Falls, Illinois, after his marriage to Charlotte Dyer, 16 years his senior. In 1880 the couple and their daughter Helen moved to California for better climate and income. In Pasadena, where Muir had been just three years before, they found about 400 people, orange and lemon groves, and a new irrigation system for a subdivision of Benjamin D. Wilson's property.

Lukens took a job as "zanjero" (tender of the ditches) for that water system, which served 32 customers. To add income, he raised fruit trees for sale and contracted to plant vineyards for other settlers. His daughter later recalled such pioneer challenges as tarantulas, dust storms, and coyotes getting into her mother's chicken flock.

Civic-minded and enterprising, Lukens soon joined in the land boom of the 1880's as Pasadena's first real estate operator. Later he fostered the public library, fought saloons, was elected Justice of the Peace, and became a successful banker. As President of the City Council for six years, Lukens was virtually "Mayor" and so escorted President Benjamin Harrison on his visit to the city in 1891. Lukens and his family lived in several substantial homes in Pasadena, the most elaborate one built on six acres of trees and gardens in 1887. It still stands today on El Molino Avenue just north of Walnut Street.

In the mid-1890's Lukens began to explore the California mountains on foot and horseback. He joined the Sierra Club in 1894, just two years after its founding in San Francisco. Soon Lukens turned his considerable energy toward trees and started a reforestation project at Henninger Flat in the mountains above Altadena. This sloping niche of nearly 40 acres had been homesteaded by William K. Henninger, who had planted fruit trees, grain, and hay. The site proved to be ideal for a tree nursery and experimental station.

Lukens and his associates believed that planting trees would improve the mountain watershed, reduce fire danger, and someday increase Southern California's annual rainfall. Even Galen Clark, former Guardian of the Yosemite Valley and Big Tree Grove, wrote to Lukens in 1904 agreeing that trees can produce climatic change and more rain. Lukens was not a trained botanist but a highly practical field observer, investigating how and where each tree species would thrive.

In 1895 Lukens was summering in Yosemite and set out for the Hetch Hetchy Valley, hoping to make the acquaintance of John Muir. Here the paths of two kindred spirits crossed when Muir appeared, fresh out of food and amiably admitting his identity to the younger explorer. From that day on, their talk of trees kept up unhindered for twenty years. And their growing friendship brought Muir back for some memorable Southland visits.

The first of these was in the winter of 1895. For a sketch of the growing town that year we turn to excerpts from the *Pasadena Star,* dated November 18, 1895:

"Pasadena Set Forth in Epigrammatic Style:
An Almost Ideal Place"

There is a city in California which *has:* Over 10,000 inhabitants; All business streets paved with asphaltum and cleaned thoroughly every night; 4 lines of railroads and trains or electric cars every 15 minutes to the metropolis 12 miles distant; Half a dozen large public schools embowered in shrubbery and of the latest style of architecture; More and finer churches in proportion to the population than any other city on the coast; Its business houses all enjoying a good trade; Just 4 policemen to keep order in the entire town; Scenic background of incomparable beauty and grandeur; [etc.; there was more]

It *has not:* Any saloon nor gambling place; A dive or anything like it; *But:* it gave this writer the worst meal ever served him in this or any other state: —Not Paradise: Pasadena!

(The author of this spirited riff was from the Bakersfield *Californian*).

A week later, the *Star* reported: "The distinguished scientist and traveler, Professor John Muir, is in the city, the guest of Councilman Lukens, president of the Pasadena National Bank. He and Mr. Lukens spent some weeks together

Muir in the Pasadena home of Lukens, about 1896. [*By permission of the Huntington Library, San Marino, California*]

this last summer in the Hetch-Hetchy Valley. Professor Muir had not been in Pasadena for twenty years and, of course, sees a few changes." Muir was to stay in town about two weeks.

On November 26, Muir and Lukens visited Echo Mountain. There Muir declared he was "greatly interested" in Professor Thaddeus Lowe's grand project of the mountain railroad and hotel, believing it would stimulate people to go to the mountains more. A few days later, on Thanksgiving, Muir had returned to the valley, but Jeanne Carr was among the crowd enjoying dinner at Lowe's Echo Mountain House and returning home by moonlight. (Just two weeks later, the *Star* reported that Galen Clark of Yosemite was himself spending the night on Echo Mountain).

While in Pasadena, Muir visited Mt. Wilson and also addressed the students of Throop Polytechnic Institute. To them he praised the importance of mountains in strengthening character. But he confided that he wished Pasadenans would visit their Sierra Madre range often "without extra inducement of a railway to pull them up." He told his audience there was no doubt that glaciers once existed in these local mountains, although their traces were nearly gone.

Muir's day-by-day activities were noted in the Pasadena newspaper of the time. But most detailed of all was the account headed: "An Evening with Muir: The Great Geologist Receives at the Home of his Friend." In the hospitable parlors of Lukens and his wife, Muir enthralled several dozen guests about "the birth of glaciers and the erosion of continents, the chimes of icebergs and the artillery of the sea." His kindly face, ever-Scottish look and voice, and almost bashful manner seemed to exert a magical hold. Jeanne Carr and Louise Conger were there that night, as were Professor and Mrs. Lowe. Afterwards, the guests went upstairs to see Lukens' collections of Indian baskets, geological specimens and other curiosities.

A few more items from the *Star* will round out our view of that memorable year, 1895. The paper reported that the "Throopites" had two victories on the football field down at Pomona College. Glasscock & Vroman (later Vroman's Bookstore) ran ads for stationery, books and Kodaks. Professor Lowe announced the opening of his "Alpine club house" (later the Alpine Tavern) at the terminus of his mountain railway. And "Pasadena's Magnificent Mooresque Palace: the Hotel Green" was newly open, with over 250 sunny rooms and the electric cars to Los Angeles passing the door.

"Great is Southern California and Pasadena is its prophet! All about it for a dollar a year in the Weekly Star." So said the subscription ad in this worthy newspaper, in that year of 1895.

John Muir and Theodore P. Lukens at Crocker Station near Yosemite, 1895 *[By permission of the Huntington Library, San Marino, California]*

In the meantime, Lukens labored strongly in his tree nursery. He walked and rode throughout the San Gabriel and San Bernardino mountains, gathering seed and observing the habits of trees. Compared to Johnny Appleseed by the *Los Angeles Times*, Lukens arranged for the planting of 53,000 seedlings (mostly Ponderosa pines) near Professor Lowe's Alpine Tavern. For Southern California conditions he also favored the knob-cone pine, which releases its seeds in fires, and the Coulter pine. In 1905, he provided some 17,000 seedling trees to the newly developed Griffith Park in Los Angeles.

Lukens was appointed Forest Agent by Gifford Pinchot, head of the new U.S. Division of Forestry and later Muir's adversary in the Hetch Hetchy controversy. When the Mt. Wilson Toll Road was widened to automobile width, Lukens was among the first to drive on it, to his forest nursery.

Muir soon brought Lukens into the Sierra Club's conservation action. The issues included government purchase of the privately-owned toll roads into Yosemite and the return of Yosemite Valley from State to Federal control. The Club was also working to protect the forest reserves from various invaders, and later to save the Hetch Hetchy valley from being dammed for an urban water supply. In 1907, Muir wrote to Lukens, "You are the man to direct & encourage the fight in the South for none know Hetch Hetchy & its surroundings so well as you do." But six long years later, that struggle was lost.

About 80 letters from Muir to Lukens are preserved in the Huntington Library today. Lukens wrote a phrase summarizing the contents at the top of each one. These letters are of brown ink, in a generously large hand with the signature

Tree nursery at Henninger Flat, about 1903 [By permission of the Huntington Library, San Marino, Calidornia]

"John Muir" extending at times five or six inches across. Their themes are of activism, political awareness, family concern, and sheer love of trees.

As the Federal government considered adding forest reserves, Muir entreated his friend, "Also write and get others to write to the Senators & Secretary of the Interior and make their lives wretched until they do what is right by the woods." As enemies of forestry tried to abolish the San Jacinto and Cleveland reserves in Southern California, Muir lamented in a letter, "the devil is in these western Senators. I wish the trees themselves could march to Congress." At the top of this one, Lukens noted "We all opposed such action & won out." Sometimes Muir simply scribbled, down the margin, "Don't forget forest salvation in general. Write to Washington people."

The two friends also corresponded in great detail about varieties of trees and their cultivation, exchanging cones and branches to be identified. Sometimes one would tell the location of noteworthy trees and urge the other to go take a look. One case was the enormous valley oaks still to be found at Fort Tejon. Lukens excitedly wrote that one was fifteen feet in diameter, and Muir promised to come—but photographs and measurements later revealed a smaller size. These oaks should not be missed today by tree lovers passing over the Grapevine at Tejon Pass.

In 1897 Lukens sent his friend in search of 400-foot Douglas spruces near Port Townsend, Washington, but all were destroyed before Muir reached there. A fallen tree was measured by Lukens at 425 feet.

Lukens also sent stacks of photographs to Muir, sometimes 100 or 200 at a time, documenting tree species and their habitats. Muir gratefully used these in articles and "for the fight" (Hetch Hetchy). The pictures aided Muir in his studies and sealed the friendship: they "will ever remind me of the trips we made on the upper Tuolumne."

In 1907, Muir visited Henninger Flat and stated approvingly "Mr. Lukens has exceeded the success of nature 100 to 1 in his experiments." When he was entertained at the Lukens' home that year and spoke of trees, the *Pasadena Star* wrote: "Pasadena's leading men and women listened raptly." Following the visit, Muir confirmed to Lukens, "It is always pleasant to think of you planting trees to grow great and do good centuries after we are all gone."

Each of the two friends was later widowed and they exchanged simple heartfelt words. Each had a daughter named

T.P. Lukens on his porch with his wife Charlotte, daughter Helen Lukens Gaut and her children, in Pasadena [*By permission of the Huntington Library, San Marino, California*]

Helen, and in 1902 Helen Lukens (later Gaut) and Muir's two girls went on a Kings River outing with the Sierra Club. Muir went to join them for a week and urged Lukens to come too; the party finally numbered about 150.

One of Lukens' last services to his comrade was to suggest a desert refuge for Helen Muir, who had recurring bouts of pneumonia. Responding to Muir's appeal, Lukens recommended the Van Dyke Ranch near Daggett and Barstow. Here Helen, to her father's great relief, grew stronger and eventually married and settled. It was here that John Muir was visiting when his last illness overtook him in 1914. The year before, he had written this in tribute to Lukens, his Southern California "fellow tree-lover": "Neither silence nor distance can abate one jot true friendship. On the contrary it glows and burns all the brighter & more divinely as we grow older."

A second friendship also enriched John Muir's Southern California stays and drew him back for return visits. Although Charles Fletcher Lummis was 21 years younger than Muir, they shared conservation interests and a peppery sense of humor. Exchanges of letters, inspiration, and family counsel sealed this unlikely friendship of two energetic characters.

Lummis was a Yankee, born in Lynn, Massachusetts, in 1859. He studied at Harvard University, bringing a precocious knowledge of Latin, Greek and Hebrew taught him by his father who was a Methodist minister. Theodore Roosevelt was a fellow student there and the two became lasting friends. After a spell of editing a newspaper in Chillicothe, Ohio, young Lummis grew restless and determined that he would go to Los Angeles—and that he would walk there. Colonel Harrison Gray Otis, publisher of the *Los Angeles Daily Times,* agreed to publish a weekly dispatch from his trek and to hire him upon his arrival.

So it was that Charles Lummis, aged 25, left Cincinnati in September 1884, walked 3507 miles in 143 days, and was welcomed by the *Times* as that "plucky pedestrian." Although there is no record that the two ever discussed their youthful ventures, Muir himself had made a thousand mile walk to the Gulf of Mexico at 29, traveling from Kentucky to Florida in 1867. Their two books on these treks—Muir's *A Thousand-Mile Walk to the Gulf* and Lummis's *A Tramp Across the Continent*—make a fascinating comparison today.

Lummis set out on a frenetically busy and productive career in Southern California. He became City Librarian of Los Angeles and soon took all of the Southwest as his canvas, in his writing and photography. He organized the Sequoya League to aid the Indian populations and the Landmarks Club to restore California's neglected missions.

He was highly influential as editor of *Land of Sunshine* (renamed *Out West* in 1902), a magazine that began as an advertising pamphlet but became a crusading voice for the Southwest. Artists and authors presented there included Mary Austin, Sharlot Hall of Arizona, Maynard Dixon, and John Muir. Lummis's own editorials were titled "In the Lion's Den" and bore this motto: "To love what is true; to hate shams; to fear nothing without; and to think a little."

As a legacy still visible today, Lummis built his own one-of-a-kind house, the stone "castle" known as El Alisal on the bank of the Arroyo Seco. Later Muir would describe this home as "the most novel and characterful and telling in every way of all I have seen this side the continent." Today it is the home of the Historical Society of Southern California, surrounded

John Muir with his wife Louie and their daughter Helen, at home in Martinez *[By permission of the Huntington Library, San Marino, California]*

by a beautiful native plant garden—a mix of wild and civilized that would have suited Lummis. High on a ridge above El Alisal rises the Southwest Museum, established by Lummis to house Indian artifacts from his own and other collections.

In the 1890's, Lummis admired Muir's essays on California mountains and asked him to write for *Land of Sunshine*. A spirited correspondence followed. Subscribing to the magazine, Muir wrote "I have read your little plucky magazine & like it. It has the ring & look of true literary metal. So has your letter to me, & I doubt not you will be successful. You have a grand field & I am sure that with honest purpose & hard work you must gain the day."

Letters by both Muir and Lummis now in the Library of the Southwest Museum trace some themes of this friendship. Writing and publishing about conservation engrossed and sometimes wearied them both. "I wish I could write as quickly & easily as most writers then you would surely get more from me than you want," lamented Muir. "But I am slow & awkward & write but little."

Lummis, on the other hand, poured out books and editorial opinion, winning this praise from Muir in 1907: "thanks for your capital Hetch Hetchy defense editorial. It's strong & every blow is called for & must tell." He added, "We are trying to stir up the thousand members of the Sierra Club to send personal letters keeping them flying thick as snowflakes in a Sierra storm, until the voice of public opinion can't be mistaken."

The 1903 rendezvous of Muir and Theodore Roosevelt in Yosemite, such a golden chance to talk of forest salvation, brought a yelp of delight from El Alisal: "…glad you are going to Yosemite with the president. Only look out that you bar

Lummis building
El Alisal, 1901
*[Courtesy of the
Southwest
Museum,
Los Angeles]*

Lummis at his
desk in El Alisal,
1904 *[Courtesy of
the Southwest
Museum,
Los Angeles]*

horses. A challenged party has the right of weapons and don't you let 'Teddy' get you to busting broncos with him. Just keep him afoot and guessing. This is really a moral obligation on you for the honor of the West." That same year Lummis himself joined Roosevelt briefly at the Grand Canyon.

To Lummis, Muir could voice his relief ("The two Calaveras groves seem safe at last") and the anger that needed outlet to a fellow writer (on the proposed Hetch Hetchy dam, "Cathedrals with dammed doors & windows would make good storage tanks & some of the dollar-people in Christ's time thought the temple a grand place for money changing.")

At times the zeal of reform proved a tiresome companion. Even Muir wearied of the many good causes urged on him by his comrade. Late in his life he wrote that he must drop "half the 20 or 30 societies" he belonged to, including some of Lummis's groups aiding the missions and Indians. Finally he complained to his friend, "Turn over a new leaf. Never a word from you these days except in a bothersome bill." But despite the grumbling, the two were undaunted in Hetch Hetchy defense until that struggle ended at last.

Lummis also helped with finding a healthful refuge for Helen Muir, when John Muir was anxiously protecting both his adult daughters. In 1905, Muir and daughters gratefully went to guest cottages in Palm Springs recommended by Lummis. There they crossed paths with Helen Lukens Gaut, their earlier walking companion in the High Sierra. By chance she was staying at the same rustic desert oasis, and she quickly telegraphed her father to join the party. They all spent six carefree days camping in nearby Andreas Canyon.

A brief newspaper piece by Helen Lukens Gaut gives an unforgettable glimpse of Muir at this desert campsite: ever in

Charles Lummis with his wife Eve, daughter Turbese, and Luis Abeita, a neighbor's son, about 1893 *[Courtesy of the Southwest Museum, Los Angeles]*

John Muir at El Alisal, photographed by Charles Lummis [*Courtesy of the Southwest Museum, Los Angeles*]

tune with his surroundings, singing "old-time songs" or standing peacefully with hands clasped behind him, indifferent to what clothes he wore but donning a flowered woolen bathrobe in evening winds, always the first one up in the morning to climb to some rocky height and "to receive the benediction of the dawn. His was the wealth of the spirit, as it is with all great men," she wrote.

Lukens and Lummis were contrasting but steadfast friends to John Muir. Lukens took himself seriously, while Lummis was famously witty, peppery, ornery. Lukens brought out sentiment in his friend, especially as they corresponded about children and about widowhood later in life; Lummis brought out Muir's humor and crankiness. Each friend provided Muir with photographs of trees or landscapes, adding dimension to the naturalist's work since he himself rarely used a camera. And each was in his own way a booster, a crusader.

With these energies Muir ardently joined. The conservation alliances he formed with these two Southlanders helped to preserve both local forests and lands beyond.

STODDARD

Hotel Maryland

✧ Chapter 3 ✧

Mountain Riches in
Public Life

TWENTY YEARS AFTER Muir's first saunter into Eaton Canyon, his Southern California experiences were taking a different turn. In the 1890's and into the new century, the mountaineer was moving onto the national stage. The carefree wanderer who had set out from Mrs. Conger's back door and returned with mountain lily bulbs was now a public figure.

A landmark in this transition was the publication of Muir's first book, *The Mountains of California*, in 1894. The book combined newspaper and magazine articles which had previously appeared, with some new material. It gave first an overview of the Sierra Nevada range, then chapters on snow, passes, lakes, forests and much more in that grand "range of light." In the final section, "The Bee-Pastures," Muir briefly revisited his San Gabriel Mountains walk of long before, recalling the bee life there among August columbines, larkspur and wild fuchsias.

By now, Muir had accepted writing as part of his mission to describe and ultimately preserve the wilderness. Although he found "wordwork" a struggle all through his life, his books brought him as a respected voice into the intersecting worlds of science, education, and politics.

The time had come for more public involvement, looking beyond the consuming ranch life of his Martinez home. In 1895, Muir wrote in his journal, "How the time flies & how little of my real work I accomplish in the midst of all this ranch work & the petty details of a domestic kind. How grand would be a home in a hollow sequoia!" The journal recounts details such as "gophers in destructive abundance," planting a hedge of Cherokee roses, making daily weather and crop notes, and roaming the hills of the ranch with daughters Wanda and Helen, talking to the plants as they went.

But in 1896 came just the opportunity Muir needed, and it would bring him again to Southern California. As a forest expert, he was asked to accompany a committee appointed by the National Academy of Sciences to study the nation's forest reserves in the West and make recommendations to the Secretary of the Interior. This welcome assignment took him with the group to Yellowstone, Idaho, Oregon and Washington, and also to the San Jacinto Range just east of Los Angeles.

The committee had distinguished members, including the academy's president Wolcott Gibbs, naturalist Alexander Agassiz, Charles Sargent of Harvard, and as secretary the young Gifford Pinchot—27 years younger than Muir, who was later the nation's Chief Forester. He was to be Muir's adversary in his last conservation battle, the proposed damming of the Hetch Hetchy Valley in Yosemite as a water source for San Francisco.

The group's final report urged forest protection and reform of grazing policies. We hear the unmistakeable voice of John Muir in the section on sheep husbandry, which condemns the pasturing of these "hoofed locusts" (Muir's own term from passionate Sierra pleas) in meadows of the Western mountains and foothills.

The report also proposed the creation of thirteen new forest reserves, and all were enacted by President Grover Cleveland in 1897. Although some states protested these restrictions on their lands, the California public was led by Muir's views to welcome its new San Jacinto Forest Reserve. (The San Gabriel Mountains, Muir's first Southern California haunt, had earlier been set aside in the Angeles Forest Reserve).

Louie Strentzel Muir died in 1905, leaving her husband with the worries of daughter Helen's frail health. Two years later Muir managed to settle Helen in Daggett, a desert hamlet close to Barstow, about 130 miles east of Los Angeles. T. P. Lukens had helped him find the spot. Also in 1907 Muir visited Henninger Flat above Pasadena and found his friend's tree nursery thriving. The link with Daggett, which continued to the end of his life, and other Southern California friendships would bring him back many times in his last years.

But first, Muir took part in two momentous happenings in Pasadena, the visits of two lions: Andrew Carnegie in 1910 and Theodore Roosevelt in 1911. His participation in these visits was a mark of his own recognition as a conservationist and as a scientist.

Pasadena was abuzz in March 1910, awaiting the private rail car from Santa Barbara bringing Carnegie, his wife and 14-year old daughter Margaret to the distinguished Raymond Hotel. The Carnegies were returning after an interval of 18 years for a nine day visit to the Crown City, Throop Institute (now Caltech), and Mt. Wilson. John Muir had been invited to join parts of their crowded schedule.

Carnegie, who was but three years older than Muir, was also Scottish born and had achieved monumental success in the American steel industry. He had retired from business in 1901 and concentrated on his philanthropic interests: Carnegie Hall in New York City (built in 1892), many Carnegie institutions benefitting science, education and world peace, and some 2,800 public libraries established in America's cities and towns.

After retirement, he lived much of each year in Scotland, a fact which must have intrigued Muir. Pride in their common ground shines out in this earlier letter from Muir to his compatriot: "To how many fine godly men and women has our stormy, craggy, glacier-sculpted little Scotland given birth, influencing for good every country under the sun!...Everybody blessed with a drop of Scotch blood must be proud of you and wish you godspeed."

"Iron Master is Jovial and Sunny," read the *Pasadena Star's* banner headline on the day of the family's arrival. "Mr. Carnegie can See Catalina Island Distinctly." From the Raymond's handsomest rooms, the party looked over the hotel's golf links (now South Pasadena apartment properties) to the blue Pacific.

Muir attended a festive luncheon for 300 guests at the Annandale Country Club, at which Carnegie declared "I consider Theodore Roosevelt the biggest man living." The Iron Master's later activities included a winning round of golf at the Raymond and day excursions as far as Long Beach, Riverside, and Redlands. Details of each day were recorded in the *Star*, some of them in the regular column for Pasadena's resort visitors, "Hotel Lobby Chat." Carnegie's humor and high spirits were mentioned many times.

Anstruther Davidson, George Ellery Hale, J.H. McBride, John Muir, H.F. Osborn, John D. Hooker, James Scherer and Andrew Carnegie at the Maryland Hotel in Pasadena, 1910 *[Courtesy of the Observatories of the Carnegie Institution of Washington]*

On March 21 the Carnegie party left for Mt. Wilson, by auto to the foot of the mountain road, then up by wagons. The Mt. Wilson Observatory had been established in 1904 through a $300,000 authorization by the Carnegie Institution of Washington, and Carnegie was eager to inspect it—in the company of its director, George Ellery Hale.

A photograph of the mountain visit shows John Muir as part of this gathering: Carnegie and Hale, James A. Scherer (president of Throop Institute, now Caltech), James H. McBride (trustee of Throop and Hale's personal physician), Anstruther Davidson (a physician and amateur botanist), and H. F. Osburn. Also with them was John D. Hooker, a Los Angeles industrialist who had given Hale $45,000 for the 100-inch mirror of the Hooker Telescope on Mt. Wilson (largest in the world until 1948) and who became a close friend of Muir. This was a constellation of Southern California figures, two distinguished Scots among them.

The next day Muir and the party attended a Los Angeles Chamber of Commerce banquet. And before the Carnegies' departure the *Star* reported two other memorable incidents. As she did on each birthday, young Margaret Carnegie gave an endowment of $5,000, this time to the children's ward of Pasadena Hospital. And the Iron Master himself visited the Pasadena Library, walking in and out unnoticed we are told, mistakenly thinking it was one of his. (South Pasadena then had and still has a Carnegie Library). Miss Nellie Russ, longtime City Librarian of Pasadena, later fussed that Mr. Carnegie would not have been proud of a 23-year old library so outgrown.

Andrew Carnegie was on his way, but Muir stayed, hoping to do some writing at his daughter Helen's home in Daggett.

John Hooker, however, persuaded him to linger a while at the Hookers' elegant house on West Adams Street in Los Angeles. There he could spread his notes in an upper room—"my palace garret" as Muir called it. He worked on his manuscript of *My First Summer in the Sierra* and enjoyed the care of Mrs. Hooker (Katherine), their daughter Dr. Marion Hooker, and Hooker's niece Mrs. Fred Jones, known to Muir as "Alice-hark-the-lark."

The Hookers were ideal friends for the widowed Muir, admiring, humorous and great travelers themselves. Katherine Hooker was the author of several travel memoirs about Italy, illustrated with her daughter's photographs, and she was a skilled bookbinder. Pictures of their home and gardens, now gone, show guests drinking tea on the fern-edged veranda, and oriental carpets tossed under the pergola for an outdoor tableau or mime.

That world is vanished now, Los Angeles before World War I. But Muir was sheltered there on several visits, later writing in "his garret" books on Yosemite and on his boyhood and youth. Katherine Hooker also introduced him to her great friend Margaret Collier Graham, wife of an early mayor of South Pasadena and an accomplished writer of fiction set in early California. Muir visited the Grahams at Wynyate, their Victorian hilltop house in South Pasadena, and according to tradition, planted a tree which grows there to this day.

In 1911, Pasadena was mad for a second major visitor, the one hailed the previous year as "the biggest man living." Theodore Roosevelt, who had finished his presidency in 1909, had just returned from an African big-game expedition and a triumphant tour through European cities. Announcing his visit, the Pasadena *Star* styled him as "Colonel Roosevelt,

Katherine and John D. Hooker with friends, on their porch on West Adams Street, Los Angeles, 1901 *[By permission of the Huntington Library, San Marino, California]*

Apostle of Justice, Civic Righteousness, World-Peace and Progress…bold, dashing and conquersome."

Roosevelt's last stay in Pasadena had been in May of 1903, as president. He had been driven down Marengo Avenue under an arch of calla lilies bearing his picture framed in red geraniums. Just a few days later that year, he was in Yosemite on May 15, having asked John Muir to meet him there. Muir had written to Charles Sargent, his colleague from the Forest Committee survey: "An influential man from Washington wants to make a trip into the Sierra with me, and I might be able to do some forest good in freely talking around the campfire."

So, escaping the usual presidential entourage, the two loquacious campers shared three days of talk with great sequoias standing by. Muir might have recalled the delight of his preservationist friend Lummis, at the challenge of keeping "Teddy" afoot and guessing. But Roosevelt, 20 years younger than his companion, stepped readily into the forest's heart and referred to the time vividly for years afterwards.

Early in 1911, Muir received a letter from James Scherer, president of Throop, inviting him to a dinner of fifteen gentlemen honoring Roosevelt on the evening before his Pasadena lecture. The naturalist John Burroughs would also be in the party, at the Orange Grove Boulevard home of Arthur Fleming, a Throop trustee.

Arriving in town on March 21, Roosevelt found the entire front page (the second page also) of the *Pasadena Star* devoted to him. The "faunal naturalist" had a busy program for his visit, including a lecture in a great canvas tent specially set up at Pasadena's Hotel Maryland on Colorado Boulevard. Rare skins, lent by local huntsmen, were placed in his suite—but

Muir in Southern California forests [By permission of the Huntington Library, San Marino, California]

no frills, just simple mahogany furniture. Even these rooms were described in detail in the newspaper.

The next day, Roosevelt spoke with boyish vigor to an audience of 2,300, the largest ever assembled in Pasadena to hear anyone. As white handkerchiefs waved, Dr. Scherer presented the speaker simply: "I introduce The American: Theodore Roosevelt." The former president, clad in swallowtail coat and pearl studs, accepted the resulting cheers, and then expressed amazement at the growth, and delight at the beauty of Pasadena.

"Dinner…brilliant," enthused the *Star* about the Fleming gathering, which included the presidents of Occidental College and Throop, as well as Adolphus Busch, millionaire brewer who lived on the neighboring property and had created Pasadena's Busch Gardens. At the center of the dinner table was a representation of a mountain, with trees on the sides and rivers dashing down.

Roosevelt proved to be a steady talker, still showing "all his usual fire." He spoke of his adventures in Africa and Egypt, and of applied sciences like those at Throop, which could yield vast projects such as the Panama Canal. Into his remarks he wove praise for all present. There was loud applause when he mentioned the books of John Muir and John Burroughs, "two eminent Johns, the great naturalists who are frequent visitors to Pasadena and are here now," said the *Star*.

Muir's journal entry for that date echoes, "it was a very brilliant and in every way Rooseveltian affair." To a Sierra Club colleague, the San Francisco lawyer William Colby, Muir reported that he had had a good long talk with TR on Hetch Hetchy matters. Roosevelt had promised his help to prevent the dam which threatened to encroach into Yosemite National Park.

For Muir, who had already received an honorary degree from Harvard and was that spring to receive one from Yale, the dinner was an affirmation of his place among leaders and academics. The young man who long ago had left college for the University of the Wilderness had graduated from its profound education with honors.

The Roosevelt dinner was another link in Muir's friendship with Burroughs, which developed largely in

John Muir and John Burroughs in Pasadena *[Department of Special Collections, University Research Library, UCLA]*

Southern California sojourns. Burroughs was just a year older than Muir, and is much less familiar to us today. Yet in the early twentieth century he was a beloved author whose essays were read by nearly every school child and whose pieces appeared in the *Atlantic* for more than sixty years.

Born in rural New York, Burroughs lived there through his lifetime and recorded its familiar landscapes and farms in essays and poems. In time he became the friend of Theodore Roosevelt, Henry Ford, Thomas Edison, Walt Whitman and others. Wherever he traveled there was a press of admirers and children bringing flowers. In 1895 he built Slabsides, a large rustic cabin on the Hudson River 80 miles north of New York City. And there that same year, John Muir came to meet him.

"A very interesting man; a little prolix at times. You must not be in a hurry, or have any pressing duty, when you start his stream of talk and adventure." So wrote Burroughs in his journal after first encountering Muir. "He could not sit down in a corner of the landscape, as Thoreau did; he must have a continent for his playground," Burroughs continued. "In California he starts out one morning for a stroll; his landlady asks him if he will be back to dinner; probably not, he says. He is back in seven days; walks one hundred miles around Mt. Shasta, and goes two and one half days without food."

The two were of different temperaments, yet were kindred spirits. Said Burroughs of his visitor, "Probably the truest lover of Nature, as she appears in woods, mountains, glaciers, we have yet had." The public knew them as "the two Johns" from then on (the western one was John of the Mountains, his friend John of the Birds).

After other visits in the East, Muir urged his fellow writer to join him in 1909 for travels in Arizona and California. Reluctant to go, Burroughs gave this description of his own essence: "The whole gospel of my books (if they have any gospel) is: 'Stay at home; see the wonderful and the beautiful in the simple things all about you; make the most of the common and the near at hand.'"

But go he did. Meeting in the Arizona desert town of Adamana, the two were off to explore the petrified forest and the Grand Canyon, then onward to Daggett and to Pasadena. Burroughs' companion and biographer, Clara Barrus, describes the household they established briefly in a rented bungalow at Lamanda Park (now east Pasadena). One day a birthday picnic was proposed for Burroughs in the Mount Lowe canyon of the San Gabriel Mountains. Other days, the three sat around a big table, each absorbed in writing; or enjoyed the appearance of *Stickeen*, Muir's dog story which came out in book form during this Pasadena visit.

Burroughs made frequent winter returns to Southern California until his death in 1921, and often Muir was able to join him. On one occasion, Pasadenans observed the two Johns walking together to the bookshop of their friend A. C. Vroman, to sign copies of their books. In 1909, the two signed the guest book of Charles Lummis at El Alisal, and Vroman added his entry to theirs: "With the big fellows I am glad to be called Friend."

Biographer Clara Barrus tells the reactions of the two naturalists when Roosevelt praised them in his Pasadena lecture. "Mr. Muir," she wrote, "who had been sitting straight as an arrow, seemed to sit straighter still, while his head seemed to lift higher and higher as the tribute progressed, and a look of unfeigned joy shone on his face; while the head of Mr. Burroughs drooped lower and lower, and, one knew, however much he wished he could hide it completely, that there were happy tears in his eyes."

But despite their differences, both thrived on Southern California experiences. In 1911, Burroughs wrote this account of visiting Mt. Wilson, looking through the telescopes there and then out over the San Gabriel Valley by night: "Another firmament down there, crowded with stars thicker than the Pleiades and much brighter. There were two large luminous seas—Pasadena and Los Angeles—connected by a narrow strait of light, and many lesser bodies surrounding them and connected with them…" Quick flashes from the trolley lines appeared to him like meteors falling below.

After John Muir's death in 1914, Burroughs continued his own winter visits. The last entry in the journal he kept for 45 years was written in Pasadena, February 1921: "Came to Pasadena Glen on the 3rd—a little bungalow called the Bluebird, snug and comfortable…life seems worth living again. Drove to Sierra Madre post office to-day. Now, at seven p.m., I hear the patter of rain." A few weeks later, he died on his homeward way, returning by train to New York.

But in 1911, the two had parted in high spirits after sharing the Roosevelt visit. Muir was off to visit grandsons ("the boy undergrowth is flourishing," he wrote to a friend). Clouds would soon be gathering, over politics and his own health, to shadow John of the Mountains. But he had always relished weather of any kind, the stronger the better..

That same year the *Atlantic* published this excerpt from his youthful journal of a Sierra summer: "Oh, these vast calm measureless mountain days, inciting at once to work and rest...Never more, however weary, should one faint by the way who gains the blessings of one mountain day; whatever his fate, long life, short life, stormy or calm, he is rich forever."

With these riches still in hand, Muir left his 1911 Pasadena sojourn ready to defend the wilderness, and to maintain his long friendships, with the old zeal.

Palm Canyon

✧ Chapter 4 ✧

Out Till Sundown

"ENDLESS SUNSHINE AND starry nights free from dew and fog," read an advertising postcard about the Van Dyke Ranch outside the desert hamlet of Daggett. "Irrigated fields, thousands of trees—brilliant ever-changing hues of the mountains—not a dude ranch but just a pleasant home-like resort for those who enjoy the desert and its arid climate—a shaded oasis in the midst of the Mojave Desert."

Here was a double appeal for John Muir and his daughters, searching in 1907 for a healthful climate for Helen who was then 21 years old. The dry air would ease her respiratory problems, which had again reached a danger point. And even desert mountains could attract at least the fleeting interest of John of the Mountains.

150 miles east of Los Angeles, Daggett was just east of Barstow. Its population then was perhaps 400, a scattered lot of miners and health seekers. Passing alongside the town, the Mojave River was as much a thought as a river, since it was often underground. Six miles to the north were the Calico Mountains, where silver had been discovered in the 1880's. Worked vigorously in the 1890's, the Silver King and Waterloo mines had yielded over 150 tons of ore in their peak year, then played out by 1896.

This activity, and a concurrent rush of borax mining, had lifted Daggett in a mini-boom. The Southern Pacific Railroad had reached town in 1882 and the famed 20-mule teams plied the desert routes there as they did at Death Valley. Perhaps $9 million in borax came from the Calico hills altogether, while some $90 million in silver was processed at the 10 stamp mill at Daggett. This mineral boom, which created also the saloons and restless population of the town, was fading when the Muirs came to the area. But the desert was ready to yield other riches—the sparse coins of solitude and of health. The arid spaces, tinted with sunset colors or brushed with whirling sands, had their own healing power.

The Van Dyke Ranch was no resort in the modern sense, but the home of Theodore Van Dyke, a Princeton graduate from a New Jersey family. He had come to the high desert climate for the health of his own lungs. His books on California landscapes were well known in the 1880's and 1890's, and he brought his law career into service as Daggett justice of the peace, carrying the title of Judge.

Theodore's brother John, a sometime visitor to the ranch, was an even better known writer whose classic work *The Desert* had appeared in 1901. This account of desert aesthetics is somewhere between geography and dream-vision. It survives well to this day—in one modern printing it joins Muir's essays in a set of literature on the American Wilderness.

Ranching for the Van Dykes was always a struggle, with the uncertain river and the rabbits getting into the alfalfa. The rainfall was probably similar to the average there today, about 4 inches per year. But the Van Dykes' cottonwood groves reached down to water, sustaining a cool island on the land.

Muir in the Southern California desert *[By permission of the Huntington Library, San Marino, California]*

Gradually a handful of people came out from the city, independent souls of various kinds, and the Judge let them build little cabins or adobes on his ranch. Botanists and artists came, and others just somehow hearing the voice of the desert. A haphazard colony of sorts turned up, amidst the creosote brush.

Here Muir and others built a little cabin for ailing Helen and her nursing companion. Her dog Stickeen and horse Sniffpony were sent down from Martinez to join her. Thus was established another link to bring Muir to Southern California until the end of his life. Daggett was to be a scene of fatherly worries and also desert discoveries in the last years of Muir's journey.

In 1907, Muir was 69 years old and two years a widower. Daughter Wanda had married Thomas Hanna the year before and they were settled into the old Strentzel adobe on the Martinez ranch. Often lonely in the big Victorian house on the property, Muir kept up a continuous thread of trips to Southern California along with other venturing in the last seven years of his life. Martinez and Daggett were the two poles of his family cares, as he hovered rather anxiously over his grown daughters.

Beyond these family centers, Muir moved during this time period in all the orbits of his energetic life. In travels, he made significant trips to Yosemite, Mt. Shasta, Arizona, and Idaho. Globally, he set off at age 73 for an eight-month trip to South America and Africa, in search of the baobab forests and other world-class trees which he eagerly reported back to friend Lukens. Academically, he was receiving honorary degrees from Harvard, Yale, the University of California and his own brief alma mater, the University of Wisconsin.

Politically, Muir carried on his conservation work to the last, including the struggle to save Yosemite's Hetch Hetchy Valley—a battle ultimately lost but which inspired a new conservation ethic for public lands (a victory snatched, perhaps, from the jaws of the dam builders). And in friendships, Muir valued the close comrades—Lukens, Burroughs, the Hooker family—and his moments with such figures as Carnegie and Roosevelt.

These were also years of productive writing, some of the best of it done in his Southern California refuge at the Hookers' home. This "pen work" he found so tedious yielded the stories of his first summer in the Sierra, the autobiography of his boyhood and youth, and his book *The Yosemite*. Notes for publishing his Alaska journals surrounded him the day he died, as a work in progress. He had just briefly put down his pen.

With all this activity, it is no wonder Muir grew tired and sometimes cranky. The wiry Scot who had once scrambled to ledges beside Yosemite Falls, to enjoy the "comets and arrows" of the dashing waters, became surprisingly frail. He lamented the damps of Martinez fogs and suffered from "la grippe." His visits to the Mojave Desert and to Helen must have benefited his own health as he checked on hers.

In the last ten years of his life, Muir had in fact sampled two desert regions. In 1905 he had taken both daughters to the high desert village of Adamana, Arizona, to ease their health. There Muir had explored the Petrified Forest six miles south (later John Burroughs joined him at this) and had noted the tough and varied plant life. His admiration went out to these survivors: sagebrush and greasewood, and the little annuals—the Indian paintbrush and desert primrose.

Ever the botanist, Muir scanned the Mojave also. Helen noted that he talked to the plants there, as he had while walking with his daughters on the two hills behind their Martinez home (hills still known as Mt. Helen and Mt. Wanda). Muir's own writings emphasize mountain flora, but he also observed the Mojave plants John Van Dyke had described this way in his book *The Desert* (1901): the salt bush that "looks the color of Scotch heather," a plant world of spines and thorns fending off danger, and the mesquite and palo verde putting forth "some bright little flag of color." These were "strange growths of a strange land!...and yet how determined to live, how determined to fulfill their destiny!"

Besides his family ties with the Southland desert, Muir was developing another bond with Southern California activists: the growing Sierra Club. In 1892 a group of 27 charter members had formed the new organization in San Francisco, to defend Yosemite National Park from being reduced in size under pressure from loggers and ranchers. The purposes of the Sierra Club would be to explore, enjoy and protect the mountain regions of the Pacific Coast—a pledge later extended to wild places across the land.

"Hoping that we will be able to do something for wildness and make the mountains glad," Muir had responded to the founding invitation. He was the unanimous choice for the first Sierra Club president. 250 people attended the first general meeting, and 500 the second a month later. In 1901 a long tradition of Sierra Club High Trips began, outings which took spirited groups of 100 or more into the mountain high country. The trips were meant to show the beauty of the wilderness so that people would work to preserve it. T. P. Lukens and his daughter Helen joined Muir and his daughter

Wanda on several High Trips, sealing their friendships with shared mountain riches.

To Muir's delight, a Southern California branch of the Club was formed in 1911, later to be known as the Angeles Chapter (today it includes all of Los Angeles County and Orange County, and is the largest of the Club's 57 chapters nationwide). Founding member Philip Bernays recorded in an oral history that he went to Pasadena to call on "Muir's friend, Mr. Vroman" at his bookstore. Vroman presented the new chapter with a set of John Muir volumes to be sent to Martinez for autographing. The set is prized today in Chapter archives in Los Angeles.

Soon the Southern Californians had trips scheduled every weekend into the San Gabriel mountains. One of their earliest activities was building Muir Lodge in Big Santa Anita Canyon, above the town of Arcadia. The rustic haven, on the way to 55-foot high Sturtevant Falls, was raised by volunteer labor and dedicated in 1913. Hikers followed an eight mile trail from the end of the streetcar line. Muir was pleased, approved the name, and sent $50. This Sierra Club haunt was enjoyed for years until the 1938 floods swept it away.

In June 1914, just before his final illness, Muir appeared unexpectedly at a Sierra Club campfire in Griffith Park. He left behind some vivid last memories of the naturalist and traveler, sitting late into the mild spring night, talking of trees in the distant South American forests he had just seen.

Meanwhile, in Daggett, Helen Muir had been married since 1909 to young Buel Funk who was the son of a ranching family there. After spending 1912 and part of 1913 in Hollywood, the couple had returned to Daggett and permanently settled just outside of town with their three sons.

Sierra Club members at Muir Lodge in Big Santa Anita Canyon about 1925 *[Courtesy of Sierra Club, Angeles Chapter]*

John Muir continued to send the young people boxes of peaches and grapes from his Martinez orchards, and wrote worriedly about his own health and Helen's.

At last he traveled south again, in December 1914. It was to be the final time. At home he had been shaping his Alaska journals into a book, working long days. The deepening winter saw him tired and ill but vividly remembering the beautiful glacier-land he had first explored thirty-five years before. To the desert he now took his notes, seeking a refuge from Martinez storms and fogs.

Arriving in Daggett on the 22nd, he found a new grandson there but also a bitter cold in the desert wind. The next day he and Helen went out walking and spoke to the plants, as of old. But his condition weakened, and that evening a doctor pronounced his case double pneumonia. Despite the risk, Muir was taken by train eighty miles to the California Hospital in Los Angeles. A local Daggett man carried the frail mountaineer aboard the train for the journey.

At the hospital (which still stands today as the California Medical Center, just south of downtown highrises), Muir rallied briefly, then died on Christmas Eve with his Alaska notebooks at his side.

Just a few years before, when he was 72, Muir had prepared for publication his journal titled *My First Summer in the Sierra*, where he had been shepherd for 2,000 sheep in mountain pastures. There he had written at age 31: "Another glorious Sierra day in which one seems to be dissolved and absorbed and sent pulsing onward we know not where. Life seems neither long nor short, and we take no more heed to save time or make haste than do the trees and stars. This is true freedom, a good practical sort of immortality."

California Hospital in Los Angeles, in the 1920s *[Courtesy of the California Hospital Medical Center Foundation]*

Thus did Muir, that Christmas Eve, cross over a border in some way, moving "onward" into the kind of immortality he recognized: becoming and remaining a part of all life.

Response to this news came quickly from Southern California friends. John Burroughs wrote in his journal on Christmas Day: "News comes of John Muir's death—an event I have been expecting and dreading for more than a year. A unique character—greater as a talker than writer; loved personal combat, and shone in it. He hated writing, and composed with difficulty though his books have charm of style; but his talk came easily and showed him at his best. I shall greatly miss him, though I saw him so rarely."

T. P. Lukens wrote simply, with a typically sentimental note: "To me he lives, as I see his many pictures before me, I can hear his voice saying some cheering word, to bring God's children into God's temple, the forests and the mountains."

The *Los Angeles Times* of December 25, 1914 declared, "All living things have lost a friend…John Muir, Apostle of the Wild, is dead." This message, they wrote, would echo through all the mountain wilds of the West. Assessing Muir's life, the *Times* found him "one of the the most remarkable characters produced by contact with the primitive West…a man of peace…and the seer of the great woods, his wonderful voice so perfectly harmonizing with the murmurs of nature." The long news article and an added commentary traced Muir's achievements in writing and in conservation.

The *Pasadena Star*, which had so long covered Muir's comings and goings, made a more personal claim. "John Muir was more than half a Pasadenan. He came here in the dawn-days of the settlement's history and roamed the mountains bulwarking Pasadena's rear, writing entrancingly of the magnificent scenery and his adventures in the wilds. He has sojourned here often and, with John Burroughs, has enriched the literary and social life of this city for weeks at a time."

A ripple of anecdotes followed in the Pasadena newspaper. One local journalist remembered calling on Burroughs in his local bungalow and finding him deep in talk about forests with Muir and Francis Fisher Browne, the editor of *The Dial* magazine, as they alternately stirred a pot of mush in the kitchen. *The Atlantic Monthly* would pay good money, she felt, for the discussion she overheard there.

Others writing in the *Star* recalled times in A.C. Vroman's bookstore in Pasadena, with Muir and friends in a back room known as "The Saints and Sinners Corner." And on Muir's opinion of the famed Mt. Lowe Railway in the San Gabriel Mountains, here is his comment to Margaret Collier Graham, South Pasadena novelist and friend: "'Tis but a scrawny thing," said Muir, "but if people will not go up the mountain except they be hauled, it may be of use." This tease, and the passionate conservation talk over a pot of porridge, seem to catch the essence of the man.

John Muir's legacy has gone far and wide by now. An Alaska glacier, a Sierra trail, a Marin County redwood grove, even several tiny plants, all bear his name. Schools, hospitals, and other establishments all over California have been named for him.

More important, the wilderness protection he fostered has been carried on and extended by the Sierra Club and many other organizations. This gift of conservation awareness was described simply by Muir's editor and longtime friend Robert Underwood Johnson: "All the other torches were lighted from his."

And what of John Muir's legacy in Southern California? In both the cities and the local mountains his name lingers. Pasadena has its John Muir High School, with a history of transformations. The name of John Muir was first used in 1913 for a junior high school in the city (T. P. Lukens wrote to his friend that year to tell him of this honor). Later, in its present Pasadena location, the school became John Muir Technical High School. Linked with Pasadena Junior College in 1938, the school was briefly known as John Muir College in the 1940's. In 1954, the campus became the John Muir High School of today. Other schools bearing the mountaineer's name may be found in Southland cities, including the new campus for John Muir Elementary School in Santa Monica, opened in 1997.

The Los Angeles Public Library provided another Muir memorial. Dedicated in 1930, the John Muir Branch at 64th

John Muir High School, Pasadena, in the 1920s *[Courtesy of the Archives of the Pasadena Historical Museum]*

Street and Vermont Avenue was a little Mediterranean-style gem, made of brick trimmed with Indiana limestone. At the opening ceremonies, Samuel Merrill of the Sierra Club, who had known Muir, told personal recollections of his friend. Several Los Angeles branch libraries were named for California historical figures in the 1930's, and this one was to have special collections on Muir and the "California out of doors."

Muir's family and early biographers sent photographs and other Muiriana to the branch, which held them for many years. Eventually, with civil unrest and earthquake damage to the building, the special Muir holdings went elsewhere for safekeeping, but the little structure is now slated for restoration.

Finally, urban explorers with sharp eyes may find recognition of Muir in unexpected places. The buildings of

Hollywood High School were constructed in 1934-38 under the WPA (Work Projects Administration), a Federal work program during the Depression. On a frieze atop the streamline moderne-style buildings were carved names of some standard heroes of Western civilization: among them, Galileo, Agassiz, Raphael, Shakespeare... and John Muir.

But Muir would have preferred to have his own legacy not in the cities but the mountains. And there we must look, into the San Gabriel range he first explored in his twenties. Two man-made structures commemorating him have been lost, but a peak remains.

The Sierra Club's Muir Lodge in Big Santa Anita Canyon, wrecked by the 1938 flooding, is long gone. But the alder-shaded canyon still offers a favorite walk for Southern Californians. Little remains of the lodge hikers enjoyed for 25 years, but you will pass the spot today en route to Sturtevant Falls.

Old photographs also show a captivating small building in the upper Arroyo Seco, the outdoor chapel at Switzer-Land (later Switzer's Camp). Here too the name of John Muir was honored. This rustic trail resort of lodge and cabins had been established by "Commodore" Perry Switzer in 1884, and it was long accessible only by foot or pack animals. In 1912, Lloyd and Bertha Austin bought the mountain camp, which later hosted such figures as Henry Ford, Shirley Temple, and Clark Gable.

The young Sierra Club often gathered at Switzer's, and they took an interest in 1924 when Austin created a little rock chapel with open air seating for 200 on the cliff side. Sierra Club leaders presented an art glass window in memory of the California mountaineers Clarence King, J. Smeaton

Chase, and John Muir. The window, according to news accounts of the time, showed scenes in the Sierra Nevada along the John Muir Trail. For years, Sunday services were held there as Switzer's Falls rushed just below.

The building of the Angeles Crest Highway past Switzer's in 1934, combined with the 1938 flood, shattered the wilderness serenity of the place. Closed at last, the resort and hillside chapel stood empty and then were demolished in the 1950's. Today, with little to show for the long history there, families enjoy picnics or camping in the forested spot still known as Switzer Trail Camp.

But mountains somehow endure, although their shapes and names may change. So it was that, in the 1940's, Sierra Club members and others looked for the crest reached by Muir on his 1877 ramble above Eaton Canyon. A rounded summit just southwest of Mt. Wilson seemed to be the spot, and it was informally named Muir's Peak in ceremonies of April 1949.

Celebrating the Sierra Club Centennial in 1992, local Club members once again "bagged" the peak. This time they brought official recognition from the Federal Government that it would hereafter be marked Muir Peak on all topographic maps. In April each year, close to John Muir's birthday, the Club organizes a convergence hike to the peak. Several groups follow different trails, approaching from all directions. Everyone is welcome to join these walks, going into the mountains to get their good tidings as Muir had urged.

"Out till sundown," John Muir once wrote about his wilderness travels. "I only went out for a walk, and finally concluded to stay out till sundown, for going out, I found, was really going in." Southern California friends knew this spirit in the man. Whether it was the conservation battle for Hetch Hetchy late in his life, a desert ramble, talking to the plants, or just that love of weather, Muir preferred to be out. "Anyplace that's wild:" that was his true home.

Muir's final sundown caught him with his wordwork still going on: his Alaska manuscript at his side. It was Christmas Eve of 1914 in Los Angeles, a city with about 320,000 inhabitants then, a new Sierra Club chapter, and the San Gabriel range as a backdrop. Beyond Eaton Canyon, Muir Peak and Mt. Wilson, the mountains rose to elevations of 10,000 feet and more. Today those same peaks and canyons invite us to explore, just as they once attracted John of the Mountains to his friendships and conservation work in Southern California.

Chapel at Switzers, Angeles National Forest *[Courtesy of the Archives of the Pasadena Historical Museum]*

Notes on Sources

Chapter 1: ORANGE GROVES AND ELFIN FOREST

John Muir's accounts of his 1877 Pasadena visit appear in his *Steep Trails* (Boston, 1918) and "The Bee Pastures" in *The Mountains of California* (New York, 1894 and many subsequent editions). The earliest published version was in *The San Francisco Evening Bulletin,* September 11, 1877. Muir frequently retold and reused bits of his writing, so the same episodes turn up with slight variations. This restless "wordwork" is a trail in itself, which may be followed in William F. Kimes and Maymie B. Kimes, *John Muir: A Reading Bibliography* (Palo Alto, 1977). The Kimes bibliography is invaluable as it comprehensively lists Muir's publications, over 500 items, with annotations, quotes, and illustrations.

See also John W. Robinson, "'A Fine, Shaggy Excursion': John Muir in the San Gabriels", *The Pacific Historian,* Vol. 23, No. 3 (Fall 1979) and William Kimes, "John Muir in Southern California", *Hoja Volante* (Zamorano Club, Los Angeles), No. 82 (November 1965).

Papers and photographs related to Dr. O.H. Conger and his family are at the Pasadena Historical Museum. So are materials on Ezra and Jeanne Carr, their son Al, and life at Carmelita. For general history of Pasadena during this period, see Hiram A. Reid, *History of Pasadena* (Pasadena, 1895). This book is scarce but worth the search, a lively work and full of personality. See also Henry Markham Page, *Pasadena: Its Early Years* (Los Angeles, 1964).

Muir's letters to Jeanne Carr are in *Letters to a Friend*, ed. William Frederic Bade (Boston, 1915). See also *The Life and Letters of John Muir*, edited by Bade (Boston, 1924). A good general biography of Muir is Frederick Turner, *Rediscovering America: John Muir in his Time and Ours* (San Francisco, 1985).

Chapter 2: TREES, FRIENDS, AND LETTERS THICK AS SNOWFLAKES

Shirley Sargent, author of many books on Sierra Nevada history, has written a brief biography *Theodore Parker Lukens: Father of Forestry* (Los Angeles, 1969). Biographies of Charles Lummis include Turbese Fiske and Keith Lummis, *Charles F. Lummis: The Man and His West* (Norman, Oklahoma, 1975) by two of his children; and Mark Thompson, *American Character: The Curious Life of Charles Fletcher Lummis* (New York, 2001). Lummis's own account of his westward trek, first published in 1892, is *A Tramp Across the Continent* (Lincoln, Nebraska, 1982).

Letters from Muir to Lukens are in the Huntington Library collections. The Braun Research Library at the Southwest Museum holds letters between Muir and Lummis. Bound volumes or single issues of Lummis's periodical *Land of Sunshine* (later known as *Out West*), which Muir admired, can sometimes be found in antiquarian book stores.

Pasadena history in fine detail, beginning in the 1890's, appears in the *Pasadena Star* newspaper on microfilm at the central Pasadena Public Library. The reminiscence by Helen Lukens Gaut is "I Remember John Muir's Visit," in the *Palm Springs Villager* (October 1948).

Chapter 3: MOUNTAIN RICHES IN PUBLIC LIFE

The 1896 forest survey group, which included Muir, wrote "Report of the Committee Appointed by the National Academy of Sciences upon the Inauguration of a Forest Policy for the Forested Lands of the United States," presented to the Secretary of the Interior and published in Washington, 1897. Further background on Southland forests is in Ronald F. Lockmann, *Guarding the Forests of Southern California* (Glendale, 1981).

The *Pasadena Star* on microfilm contains many details of Carnegie's and Roosevelt's visits to Pasadena.

Papers and photographs related to the John Hooker family and their Los Angeles home are in the Huntington Library collections, as are the travel books written by Katherine Hooker. The life of John Burroughs, including his friendship with John Muir and photographs of the two, is traced in Clara Barrus, *The Life and Letters of John Burroughs,* 2 vols. (Boston and New York, 1925) and Clara Barrus, *Our Friend John Burroughs* (Boston and New York, 1914). Barrus also edited *The Heart of Burroughs's Journals* (Port Washington, N.Y. 1928).

Chapter 4: OUT TILL SUNDOWN

For background on the Muirs' years in Daggett, see Peter Wild's articles "John Muir and the Van Dyke Ranch: Intimacy and Desire in his Final Years, Parts 1 and 2," in the *John Muir Newsletter,* published by the University of the Pacific,

Stockton (Summer 1995 and Fall 1995). See also John C. Van Dyke, *The Desert* (Salt Lake City, 1980).

The founding of the Sierra Club is described in the Club's illustrated Centennial volume, Tom Turner's *Sierra Club: 100 Years of Protecting Nature* (New York, 1991) and also in Michael P. Cohen, *The History of the Sierra Club, 1892-1970* (San Francisco, 1988). The archives of the Angeles Chapter of the Sierra Club are in the Department of Special Collections, University Research Library, UCLA.

The history of the California Hospital, which opened in 1898, has been written under its current name: see Addison C. Bennett, *A Lantern of Hope: the History of California Medical Center—Los Angeles* (Los Angeles, 1993).

Finally, the indispensable source for history of the local mountains Muir traversed is John W. Robinson, *The San Gabriels: Southern California Mountain Country* (San Marino, 1977) and his *The San Gabriels II: The Mountains from Monrovia Canyon to Lytle Creek* (Arcadia, 1983).

✧ Voices from the Past ✧

These original source materials bring us the words of John Muir and his friends, in their correspondence and reminiscences of time spent together. The newspaper accounts describe his visits in the Southland, and the obituaries reflect on his place in the world and also in the region where he spent his last days: Southern California.

✧ From Muir's Correspondence with T. P. Lukens ✧

Martinez, Dec. 28, 1898

My dear Mr. Lukens—

I thank you heartily for the magnificent lot of forest photographs just arrived. Few could guess that so many grand pictures of forest, [wild] garden & mountain could be found in San Bernardino Range.

I got home about a month ago. Spent the summer in New England, Canada & the Southern States studying the forests & of course I had a grand time especially in the Alleghenies. The forests there of oak, maple, hickory, Linden, Magnolia, Liriodendron, Oxydendron, Tupelonyssa etc. are perfectly glorious. I'm trying to write about them.

Our Sierra Club seems half dead & I don't know but you South Cal people will have to start another Alpine forest club.

With many thanks, wishing you all a Happy New Year I am ever Yours,

John Muir
Love to Lottie [Lukens' granddaughter]

Martinez, Dec. 26,1900

My dear Mr. Lukens:

I thank you heartily for the handsome book of photographs which I know cost much pains & time & money. How well they illustrate your long delightful wanderings especially in the Sierra & San Gabriel. Apart from the beauty & the friendliness it shows, it will be ve₁y useful to me in my studies & ever remind me of the trips we made on the Upper Tuolumne. I wish I could send you something that would give you anything like as much pleasure. Remember me with best wishes of the New Year to Mrs. Lukens & Lottie. I hope she will like the little book I picked out for her. Come & see us.

Ever Yours,

John Muir

Martinez, Apr. 13, 1902

Dear Mr. Lukens:

I took great pleasure in forwarding the check you sent me to Sec. Colby for membership in the Club & for the Kings River Outing for Mrs. Jones. No doubt she will enjoy it. My two girls are going & I have promised to be with the party for a week at least. I hope you also will manage to be with us. Mr. Colby tells me the party will be quite large, perhaps 150 or more.

With best wishes for you all I am

Cordially Yours,

John Muir

William Colby had been appointed Sierra Club secretary in 1900 and "invented" the High Trips, taking large numbers of Club members into the Sierra Nevada range each summer. Mrs. Jones was T. P. Lukens' daughter Helen, whose first husband was E. E. Jones.

Martinez, Jan. 22, 1907

Dear Mr. Lukens:

As you suggested I have written a letter for the meeting to celebrate [Robert] Burns' birthday [in Pasadena] & have sent it today by registered mail to Mr. McDonald. If it is to be read at the meeting I hope the reader has a gude Scots tongue in his head.

With best wishes,
Faithfully yours,

John Muir

Martinez, Dec. 12, 1907

Dear Mr. Lukens:

I think I told you that Helen had another attack of pneumonia about two months ago. She is slowly recovering & is able to go around the house but the rains & fogs of the last few days have made the weak lung sore & the doctors say as I do that she must go again to the desert & stay for two years, at some ranch where milk, eggs, vegetables, etc. can be had. Do you know of any such place—say about Barstow or Mohave or indeed anywhere. Perhaps Mr. Gaut in his extensive travels may have found such a place available for a merry though sick boarder & her anxious old father.

How are you all, well I hope. Have you seen the Sellers lately? Sick or well I am faithfully yours,

John Muir

James Gaut was Helen Lukens' second husband. The Sellers were mutual friends of Muir and Lukens.

Martinez, Mar. 11, 1908

Dear Mr. Lukens:

I have been very sick but am up & slowly convalescing—
hoping soon to get into the Sierra for a breath of reviving air.
I had a severe attack of the grippe (the 3rd this winter) & it
came near making an end of me. The last four years have been
full of anxiety & sorrow & sickness making me barren &
useless. But I must not complain for most of my life has been
joyous & free above most. Thanking you for your kind
sympathy I am ever faithfully your friend,

John Muir

On a Postcard, showing a forest view in "Lembranco do Jardim Botanico", sent from Rio de Janeiro, Brazil.

Jan. 11, 1913

Dear friend & fellow tree lover—
I heartily wish you & your blessed family a happy new year. How are you these troubled destructive progressive days? Bravely well I hope. With all good wishes ever your friend,

John Muir

Martinez, Sep. 20, 1913

Dear friend Lukens:

Neither silence nor distance can abate one jot true friendship. On the contrary it glows and burns all the brighter & more divinely as we grow older.

I know well how you feel for your tree family on the mountains, the right kind of wealth ever blessing yourself with their life-giving beauty & shade, & innumerable others now & hereafter who will bless you in turn & truly keep your memory green.

Remember me to all your family.

Write to Senators & the President [Wilson] protesting against Hetch Hetchy bill especially Poindexter & Smoot.

Ever faithfully,

John Muir

✧ From Muir's Correspondence with Charles Lummis ✧

Martinez, Mar. 24, 1900

My dear Lummis,

Many thanks for your editorial in last Sunshine [*Land of Sunshine*]. The two Calaveras Groves seem safe at last. Now we must fight for a decent administration of parks & reservations in general on a permanent basis. Only the merest beginning has been made. In particular the appropriations for forest guards & rangers are ridiculously inadequate.

I should like very much to see you but the way seems blocked just now with work that should have been off my hands long before this. Of miserable interruptions there has been no end this winter. How you can accomplish so much is to me marvellous. Good luck to you. Come to my house when you can. Possibly I may be your way within six months but I dinna ken.

Cordially yours,

John Muir

Martinez, Apr. 3. /01

My dear Lummis,

Many thanks for the good book & photos. They are all good. Mrs. M likes the side views best. I should like to get a doz. or so of each including the one with the dog sitting & the desk & if you will get them printed I'll send cash for the work.

I've been reading the Corners [*Some Strange Corners of Our Country*] & find them capital. Don't waste time on small or even big passing squabbles when you can do lasting things like these books.

We all remember your visit with pleasure. Love to the small wildling [Lummis' daughter Turbese].

Ever Yours,

John Muir

Martinez, Apr 9 /01

My dear Lummis,
I want
one doz. copies of desk
" " " " dog seated
none jumping
" " " " each of the others
Half of them mounted, all unvarnished, on rough paper.

Your fight love reminds me of the good man in Job, 29th Chap. who among other benevolent things "broke the jaws of the wicked" and of Scotch schoolboys whose main ambition was to be "gude fechters." My own bloody nose & black-eye battles averaged about three or four a week.

Faithfully Yours

John Muir

Martinez, March 18, 1902

My dear Lummis,

Here is ten dollars for your poor Indians. I feel sure that now something sensible & brotherly will be done for them.

How kindly you noticed my little outdoor book! Such words of sympathy & insight from one who can write means something real & fine. Many thanks.

Remember me to the little wild lassie [Turbese] & believe me ever sincerely yours,

John Muir

Martinez, Apr 28, 1902

I have to go to Kings River Yosemite next June to help the Sierra Club outing, thence to the Upper Kern—can't go with the Canon [Grand Canyon] party, but hope you can, as guide missionary eye-opener & friend. I was at Bright Angel last January to get a glimpse of the Canon in winter garb—made one trip to the bottom, rode & sauntered thirty or forty miles along the rim, gazed & dreamed on gable & promontory, watched dawns & sundowns, etc. & enjoyed two small snow storms. The flight of the snow & the coming & going of the clouds were glorious— but so is everything. A few years ago I made the trip by stage from Flagstaff & went down the Hance Trail to the River & I have seen something of the head fountains in the Rockies, but its all untellable, unspeakable. Yet I was fool enough to try to write about it after years of editorial prodding & am still trying. The job is rightly yours, but wiser than I, excepting a few clarion cockcrows, you have held your wheest most ably.

You had just been to the Canon with the Ripley party & I had no hope of getting you to go with me in January. Still I look forward to a grand trip in that glorous region with you, visiting the Petrified Forest, old cities, etc, just our two selves, for I want to make your acquaintance & this is the only way.

With love to Turbese I am,

faithfully yours,

John Muir

April 25th 1903

Dear John Muir:

I hope the "Glaciers" have by this time made their way to the encyclopedic sea and broken off and drifted away leaving you foot-loose. I have just this morning mailed my article on California to the same office—and it has made me hump this week to put so much California into so small a pinhole as ten thousand words.

I am mighty glad you are going to the Yosemite with the President [Theodore Roosevelt], part of my consolation being that he can't lose you as easily as he did Brother Burroughs [John Burroughs] in the Yellowstone. Only look out that you bar horses. A challenged party has the right of weapons and don't you let "Teddy" get you to busting broncos with him. Just keep him afoot and guessing. This is really a moral obligation on you for the honor of the West. I want him to find that even the Jeremiahs out here can stay with him all day. I wish I could be a fly on a redwood stump while the procession goes by. I am going over to the Grand Canon about the 2nd and see if we can pull it up a little nearer the surface so that he can explore the whole business in nine hours besides shaking hands with the whole population of Arizona. I hear that numerous suspicious looking boxes whose contents are not necessarily for publication but as a guarantee of good faith are being sent to the Grand Canon Hotel in my name to be presented to the President; but I am forming a dark plan to open those boxes just before he gets there and encourage the assembled population of Arizona to take his health so heartily that by the time of his arrival they will all be sitting down and leave him foot-loose. Don't you think this would be justifiable?

Your program does not look very encouraging but I shall continue to hope that after all you will squeeze out two or three days to roll in and see me before exposing yourself to the dangers of nervous prostration among the tenderfoot circumnavigators.

Turbese sends her love to all of you.

Hastily but

Always your friend

Charles Lummis

Palm Springs, Cal.
June 13 /05

Dear Mr. Lummis—

You made no mistake in sending us here. The water is cool and delightful, as are the nights. The days [are] hot enough and dry enough to evaporate every disease and all one's flesh. On our arrival the first night we lay down under the olive tree in the sandy orchard, and the heat of the sand brought vividly to mind Milton's unlucky angels lying on the burning marl. But O the beauty of the sky evening and morning and how charming the old doctor and his wife. Helen is better already. [Muir's daughter]

Your June number is first rate [*Out West*, which had formerly been named *Land of Sunshine*]. Charlotte [i.e. Sharlot] Hall's Arizona article is capital.

With kindest regards to Mrs. Lummis and the children and Moody, in which we all join, I am

Faithfully yours,

John Muir

[FROM CHARLES LUMMIS]

Apr. 29th 1906

Dear Muir:

It is a long time since we have had any word from you, and I don't know whether you were in the earthquake belt or where. Naturally we feel anxious. If this comes to your hand, will you not please let us know as soon as possible where you are, and what you are, and who you are, and what the thunder you are doing.

I have been in bed for days trying to have pneumonia, but am about to give it up in disgust.

When you come this way again, please bring me a full-sized Sequoia for my Library Roof-garden.

Remember us all to the girls.

With love,

Always Your Friend,

Charles Lummis

Martinez, Nov. 4 1907

Dear Mr. Lummis:

Many thanks for your capital Hetch Hetchy defense editorial. It's strong & every blow is called for & must tell. Keith [William Keith] & I got back two weeks ago from a camp trip to Hetch Hetchy Yosemite & our grand old artist was charmed by it into newness of life. He made 38 sketches, & declares that in fine picturesque park beauty it surpasses Yosemite. There is a short article of mine in the Outlook for Nov. 2d which though not illustrated will give you something like a general picture of the Valley as it is & would be if drowned.

We are trying to stir up the thousand members of the Sierra Club & as many other lovers of God's mountain handiwork as we can reach to send our protests to Washington in the form of personal letters to the Secretary & President, keeping them flying thick as snowflakes in a Sierra storm, until the voice of public opinion can't be mistaken. Light is all that's needed to defeat the plans of these cunning money-changers & water-changers.

The mountaineering clubs of Oregon are coming to our help, so is the Appalachian. I have no news from Washington good or bad except one encouraging letter from the President.

If successful in getting large enough appropriations for a good wagon road into the Valley & a trail up the big Tuolumne Canon the salvation of the glorious Hetch Hetchy will be made sure for then it will be seen & known by countless thousands, making effective lying impossible.

Remember me to Mrs. Lummis with kindest regards & to your little son & daughter & believe me,

ever faithfully yours,

John Muir

Helen Lukens Gaut was the only child of Theodore P. Lukens. She enjoyed a number of outings with John Muir and his daughters, one of which is described in the article below. She published many magazine pieces, stories, poems and songs which sold well. In particular, her articles on Southern California gardens and homes give a vivid record of architecture and the life of her time. Her work deserves rediscovery, and perhaps her songs will be sung once again.

Palm Springs Villager, October 1948

I REMEMBER JOHN MUIR'S VISIT

By Helen Lukens Gaut

In the summer of 1905, John Muir, famous author, discoverer of Muir Glacier, grand old man of forested mountains and alpine lakes, arrived in Palm Springs, a prayer in his heart that the health of his younger daughter, Helen, might be benefited by the hot dry air of the desert.

A telegram to Dr. Welwood Murray, relayed from the railroad station, informed him that John Muir and daughters, Wanda and Helen, would arrive on the afternoon train, and requested transportation and accomodations at his hotel which had been closed for the summer. The guest cottages were deep with dust from recent sand storms. Dr. Murray was in a dither of excitement. He ran his fingers through his touseled white hair and beard. Perspiration oozed from the age-deep lines on his troubled face. Then suddenly, himself a recognized scholar and philosopher, an eccentric blustering old Scotchman with the roar of a lion and the heart of a dove, went into action.

Mrs. Murray, handicapped by overweight and increasing deafness, was somewhere in the garden. She had never failed him in times of stress and anxiety.

"Elizabeth!" he shouted.

No answer.

"Lizzie!"

Still no reply.

Then "LIZ" in a thunderous voice.

With this final summons she appeared with a basket of freshly picked grapes and figs, her face a patient map of questioning. Explosively, he explained, "The Muirs are coming. Three of them. They're coming today."

"But we cant—" Dismayed at the prospect of house cleaning, of cooking and serving meals, Mrs. Murray, near collapse, deposited her 180 pounds on a bench, arguing against—but trying to plan.

For several days I had been camping on the bank of the zanja in Dr. Murray's garden oasis. Having previously camped with the Muirs in Paradise Valley in the High Sierras, I was overjoyed with the prospect of seeing them again, and offered to help in any way I could. Dr. Murray accepted my offer, but rather dubiously, apparently doubting that a young woman writer could be of much use. It was only because of my father's (T.P. Lukens) notable work in reclamation and reforestation, that he tolerated my being there at all during the closed season. In his present dilemma, I decided, was my opportunity to win the approval of this old Scotchman.

In a paroxysm of haste he dashed across the road to the Caliente Reservation, returning speedily with Ramon, a stalwart young Indian, and Amada, gowned in a voluminous calico mother-hubbard. Given brooms, mops, buckets and soap, Dr. Murray ordered them to "exterminate the superfluous accumulation of dirt." One of his pet hobbies was to familiarize the Indians with the niceties of the English language.

I was told to ride with Marcus, a patriarchal Indian, grey as the sage, bronzed as the hills, to meet the Muirs at the station. The so-called stage—a rickety, heat-shrunken uncovered wagon, was dragged through the six miles of sand by two antiquated mustangs. The Muirs' luggage, along with boxes of freight billed to Dr. Murray, which I hoped contained provisions to supplement storekeeper Bunker's meager supplies, were hoisted into the wagon box.

Mr. Muir and daughter, Helen, climbed to the high seat beside Marcus, the hoary apostle of desert silence. Muir's blue eyes were bright with anticipation. His brown hair and beard were but slightly grey at 60.

Wanda and I sat on a board that rested precariously on the sides of the wagon box and away we went, the wagon creaking and swaying in the deep wheel ruts that marked the road through drifting sand. A desert wind, increasing in velocity, stabbed us with dagger-like pellets of sand. In the open-jawed spaces, outside shelter of Mt. San Jacinto, in an out-of-doors new and strange to him, Mr. Muir had the opportunity to compare this maniac wind with the clean crisp tempests he'd met with in his beloved forests. With the desert in a state of hysteria, talking was impossible, and so we sat huddled and silent until we reached the oasis of Palm Springs.

Guest cottages had been made ready; pitchers of fresh water, bowls, towels and soap on the wash stands; baskets of figs, grapes, oranges and grapefruit on small tables. Mrs. Murray had contrived a plain but appetizing meal to be ready on the long board table in the adobe dining room.

During the meal the two opinionated old Scotchmen had a lively talkfest, exploding their theories, sometimes in cordial agreement, sometimes in heated argument. Mr. Muir, naturally gentle, kindly, and unobstrusive, expressed, but definitely, his belief in Dr. Murray's theory of geological evolution. Dr. Murray's voice rose in a roar of disputation, banging his fist on the table until the dishes rattled. Finally peace was restored when Muir quietly remarked with his inimitable chuckle, "Rocks are rocks—no matter how they evolved."

Dinner finished, Murray glanced worriedly at the litter of dishes, then at his wife. "She hasn't been well," he said, "and..."

Wanda, young, strong, efficient in any emergency, said "Don't worry. We'll manage." She started clearing the table and went into the kitchen, from which came a terrified scream and crash of broken crockery. Rushing out we found her in the center of the litter, eyes bulging with horror at crickets, big black ones, on the sink, others crawling up through the cracks in the old floor boards. Murray assured her they were quite harmless, while her father, with his inimitable chuckle, remarked "For shame! To think a daughter of mine could be scared and let out such a yell because of a few little beetles."

For several days, Wanda, in spite of her antipathy for the bugs, took complete charge of the cuisine.

Star-bright evening hours were spent in the palm-thatched pergola over the rugged pillars of which were vines heavy with clusters of purple grapes. The night air in contrast with the intense heat of the day, was cool, and drifted with fragrance of oleander ad orange blossoms. In this rare botanical garden were trees, vines and shrubs which had been shipped to Murray from far corners of the world for experimental planting in the desert.

Muir's contentment was evident. His voice was low, leisurely as a woodland brook, as he talked on and on of his adventures in the out-of-doors; weaving rare word pictures of rugged peaks, deep canyons, waterfalls, glaciers, wildflower meadows and cathedral forests.

One had only to press the electric button of his anecdote generator to make him drift into reminiscence.

Asked why he tramped alone into far-away wildernesses, he said, "Because of my reverence for God's country, for the wealth of beauty and perfectness I find there. When tired, I brew a cup of tea, nibble on crackers or dry bread, lie on a carpet of pine needles, a mossy bank. a flat-topped rock, or a slab of glacial ice—then feast on the scenery. Afraid? What of? I'd rather climb a mountain peak or scale a glacier in dead of night than cross a city street and dodge traffic in broad day. That's the only time I am really scared."

Muir was slender, almost frail in appearance. It seemed a gust of wind would blow him over. But he was like a reed— strong, capable of meeting any need for physical endurance. His shaggy beard, streaked with grey, gave him the look of an old-time school master. In conversation, as in all his writings, he believed in simplicity of expression. A spade was a spade, not an agricultural implement. He had a keen sense of humor.

One morning when hearing Murray instruct Ramon how to plant trees in language such as this: "You must make the excavations of greater radius at the lower extremities than at the upper, in order that the wide spreading roots will have greater opportunity for expansion."

Muir chuckled with amusement and said: "Murray's confusing that poor Indian with those big words. What in thunder does Ramon know about radius and extremities of expansion? Why not tell him to dig a hole. He'd understand that."

One day Murray broached the subject of ideals. "Ideals, fiddlesticks!" Muir exclaimed. "John Burroughs got off some foolishness about ideals. As for me, I just jog along enjoying every sheaf of grass, every blossom, every sunbeam, every rain cloud."

For several days the thermometer ranged from 100 to 120. Wanda, burdened with her self-appointed task of cooking, along with her continuing antipathy for crickets, began to show signs of wilting. To make things easier for her, Murray suggested having picnics in some of the canyons, where cooling streams and deep shade would be respite from the heat. His plan was met with cheers of approval. So into the old wagon went a basket of provisions, along with pillows for Helen, for whom he'd taken a great liking. Nothing was too good for her. She must have every comfort.

Murray took the reins. Helen sat on the "prescribed" pillow between him and her father. Wanda sat behind on a board. With a flip of the whip to awaken the horses, with me astride an Indian pony "Whirlwind," we were off for Palm Canyon, seven miles from the village. And what a road! Narrow, deep with sand in places, or punctuated with huge boulders over which the wagon wheels had difficulty in straddling. We hadn't gone far until Helen insisted on changing places with me. In spite of Murray's vigorous objections, his declarations that such violent exercise would be the death of her, she had her merry way—as she usually did—, mounted Whirlwind and dashed ahead in a cloud of dust, while I tok her place on the seat elbow to elbow with Murray, who for some minutes was too angry and frustrated to speak.

Muir thought the incident a huge joke and whispered to me: "Now's your chance to make him like you." As I had previously confided to Muir my failure to quite win Murray's friendship, he quietly voiced this advice: "You must learn how to approach a Scotchman. Why don't you exert your charming feminine ways? There is a lot of good—even in a Scotchman."

Reaching the mouth of the canyon, Helen dismounted, removed the saddle and led her horse to the stream to drink. She seemed in fine mettle after her invigorating ride. Muir was overjoyed at her improvement in health, and sprinted with youthful enthusiasm as Murray led us up a steep trail densely hedged with cacti, then down into the scenic rock-tumbled bed of the canyon.

Muir was more interested in this miracle nature growth than in the excellent lunch Wanda had prepared. In answer to his questioning, Murray said: "No one knows their origin. They are believed to be hundreds of years old. The Indians regard them with reverence, and have woven many legends about them."

Returning, we circled around through the "Garden of Eden," where a few tumble-down shacks were all that remained of a fantastic dream of real estate promoters to develop and build a world-renowned city, even going so far as to run a street-car railway to connect their dream city with the railroad station ten miles distant. A long abandoned car half buried in sand, remained then as monumnetal evidence of the ill-fated project.

Our next picnic was held in Tahquitz Canyon beside a rainbow-misted waterfall, a gallant stream rushing down from the forested heights of Tahquitz mountain. The Indians, Murray informed us, believed this mountain to be the home of the devil, who, during an earthquake, would emerge in full regalia of stovepipe hat and tails, and carry off their most beautiful maidens.

In the shadowy cool of twilight hours, Muir delighted in strolling through the meadow at the base of San Jacinto, along the stone-walled zanja which at that time supplied water for the Village and reservation. He'd stand in reverent silence beside the weather-scarred wooden crosses in the old cemetery. He found much of interest in studying Indian psychology when visiting the palm thatched fiesta hut on the reservation, where tribal feasts and religious ceremonies were held.

Wanda and Helen experienced many a thrill when bathing in the hot mineral spring that gurgled from unknown depths, its water so buoyant, one had to cling to a wooden cross-beam to avoid popping up like a cork. The spring and rickety bath-house belonged to the Indians who charged twenty-five cents for a dip.

As a solution to Wanda's culinary difficulties Muir decided it would be a fine idea to leave the hotel and camp in one of the canyons during the remainder of their stay. Murray stubbornly opposed this plan, declaring that roughing it, sleeping on the ground, would never do for little Helen. Then, realizing Muir's mind was made up, that both Wanda and Helen were eager for a change, he suggested that Andreas Canyon, dense shaded with a running stream, and only three miles from the Village, would be an ideal location, and set about packing blankets, provisions, and pots and pans.

My father, T.P. Lukens, connected with the U.S. Division of Forestry, had arrived in response to an urgent telegram from Muir, requesting he join us in the outing. A young man employed by the Biological Survey in Washington, D.C. to collect desert specimens, had also arrived.

Old Marcus helped unload on the bank of a brave little stream that went singing through a tangle of wild grape vines, alders, cottonwoods, and a small isolated group of palms.

Immediately Muir stepped from the wagon, he was reverently, quietly in tune with his surroundings. For some time with hands clasped behind him—a characteristic posture—he studied the far-reaching vistas of sand wastes below us, where shadows and brilliant sunset colors mingled in kaleidoscopic confusion. Turning, he faced the canyon walls that soared to great height, where jumbled boulders gleamed like polished brass. Gazing at this nature phenomenon born ages ago, he remarked: "Definite evidence of glacial energy! I wish Murray was here with me. I'd prove to him..."

Meanwhile we spread blankets on the mattress-like layer of dry leaves, cleared space among the rocks for a camp fire, hung baskets of provisions to tree branches beyond reach of ants, and in a tin container anchored butter, eggs, bacon and cheese in the stream for refrigeration.

Six carefree days passed all too swiftly—evenings around the camp fire singing the old-time songs best loved by Muir; listening to his stories of travel and adventure; hearing my father tell of his work of reforesting our fire-denuded mountain slopes with young trees grown at the government station at Henniger Flats above Pasadena; while the "U.S. Bug Man" as the girls had dubbed him, recounted his trapping experiences, of feasting on woodchuck roast and rattlesnake fries.

Regarding clothes Muir was indifferent. Any old suit would do. Here on the desert he wore white linen or grey alpaca made from materials he'd bought in India. His one treasured garment was a long woolen bath robe splashed with gay-colored flowers. This he wore when chill evening winds came down from the high meadows. Having no worries about shaving, of the color of his neckties or the fit of his clothes, gave him leisure to enjoy nature, time to write the word-pictures of out-door beauty to be found in each and every chapter of his many books. In his self-effacement he eliminated the personal pronoun in his endless chain of anecdotes.

In contrast to his usual quiet calm, he did, one day, startle us with a blood curdling yell, danced around and shook a big red ant out of his breeches instead of a centipede or scorpion he'd suspected was making a meal off his "hind leg," as he described his lower extremities. "That ant," he said with a chuckle, "knew I had no business here, so tried to scare me to death."

"To think," Wanda teased, "that a father of mine could be scared of a poor little ant."

He found many plants he'd met with in the deserts of Nevada and Utah while with the Geodetic Survey in 1876. He was greatly interested in studying Indian hieroglyphics on the rock walls of a nearby cave.

Muir was always first to get up in the morning, leaving quietly to avoid disturbing the rest of us, and climb to some rocky height to receive the benediction of the dawn. His was the wealth of the spirit, as it is with all great men.

The Pasadena Star of March 22, 1911 held three full pages detailing former President Theodore Roosevelt's visit to the city. The flurry of headlines and sub-heads included these: "Col. Roosevelt Is Vigorous As of Old"; "Beginning to Show Some Age but Still Has All His Usual Fire;" "Stops to Talk with Children"; "Given Ovation by Crowds on Streets as He Comes to Pasadena"; "Audience of 2300 Greets Him at Lecture." And also this: "Dinner Given by Mr. Fleming is Brilliant."

John Muir was among the guests at this party, given at the Orange Grove Blvd. home of Arthur Fleming, Canadian-born lumber tycoon and self-made millionaire, a long-standing Trustee of Throop Polytechnic Institute (now the California Institute of Technology). The gathering consisted of 15 men, and it was reported in the Star as follows:

The *Pasadena Star*, March 22, 1911

As soon as the former President had gone into his room [at the Hotel Maryland] and shut the door, his private secretary guarded the portal zealously, so that nobody should disturb him. Reporters thronged outside. Some wanted to interview him, others to take a flash-light photograph of him amid the beautiful surroundings provided by Mr. and Mrs. D. M. Linnard. To all Frank Harper turned the stony face, proving an ideal private secretary and enabling Mr. Roosevelt to get some rest before he went off with Dr. Scherer to the house of A. H. Fleming on Orange Grove Avenue, where he dined.

The other guests numbered thirteen, but Roosevelt made the fourteenth, and the host the fifteenth man, so there was nothing unlucky about the banquet. The guests were: Mr. Roosevelt, Meyer Lissner, chairman of the Los Angeles general committee, E. T. Earl, General Adna R. Chaffee, General M. H. Sherman, Dr. Norman Bridge, John Burroughs, John Muir, Dr. James A. B. Scherer, Adolphus Busch, James Culbertson, Dr. Robert J. Burdette, Eldridge M. Lyon and Dr. John Willis Baer of Occidental College.

Decorations at Dinner

The feature of the decorations on the dining table at the Fleming residence was a representation of a mountain, with trees on its sides and rivers dashing down. The floral embellishments consisted of nothing but orchids, of which there were a dozen varieties. Mr. Roosevelt proved himself to be the freshest and the most boyish man of those present. [T.R. was then 53 years old, 20 years younger than John Muir.] Nobody would have thought he had been through a strenuous day or had the Throop lecture before him. He appeared even younger than Meyer Lissner, whose boyish looks have been a matter of surprise to all politicians.

Mr. Roosevelt eagerly discussed with General Chaffee projectiles, both for military and sporting purposes; he and Adolphus Busch were on common ground when they talked of African scenes and places because the multi-millionaire brewer has seen almost as much of what used to be called the "dark continent" as has the former President. With Muir and Burroughs, two great old friends, the former chief executive talked with great gumption. He said one of the finest trips he ever had was into the Yosemite with Muir. Roosevelt seemed to be almost an incessant talker at the banquet, and on every subject brought up he seemed to know a great deal; in fact he spoke almost as an expert. No matter what the topic, he knew something about it and he proved himself to well bear the reputation of being a great conversationalist. He showed no sign of fatigue nor exhibited any listlessness, and appeared to enjoy himself in every way.

The other gentlemen present were: Lissner, of Los Angeles; Earl; Chaffee; Sherman, who had built the first electric inter-urban rail lines in Southern California ; Bridge, a Chicago physician retired to Pasadena for his health, and a generous supporter of Throop Polytechnic Institute; Burroughs, naturalist, author, and friend of Muir; Scherer, president of Throop Polytechnic Institute; Busch, prominent brewer who wintered in Pasadena and created the famous Busch Gardens on his Arroyo Seco land; Culbertson, a lumber merchant and a Trustee of Throop; Burdette, author, civic leader, and pastor of Temple Baptist Church; Lyon; and Baer, president of Occidental College.

December 25, 1914

Dust to Dust

EARTH HE LOVED RECLAIMS HIM

———

John Muir, Apostle of the Wild is Dead

———

Famous Naturalist Stricken by Pneumonia

———

Body to be Taken North for Funeral Sunday

———

JOHN MUIR IS DEAD

Up through the far-flung reaches of the Yosemite, the Sequoia, the Muir Woods and all the mountain wilds of the West will ring the mournful echo of that message, for the birds and the beasts and all living things have lost a friend.

America has lost perhaps its greatest naturalist, the world one of its most remarkable nature poets.

John Muir died of double pneumonia at the California Hospital yesterday morning and until his death released the great soul few even knew that he was in Southern California.

Possessing a wonderful fund of information gathered during all the years of his wanderings among the wilds of the world, Mr. Muir was a slow producer; yet the books and stories he has written stand out in bold relief on the best bookshelves of the world. It was while he was polishing and repolishing his book on Alaska, at his home in Martinez, that the strain and overwork reduced his vitality. He laid aside the pen and left for Daggett, where his daughter, Mrs. Buel A. Funk, resides, in the hope that a change of air would bring relief.

Dr. McKenzie of Daggett sent for Dr. George L. Cole of Los Angeles last Monday. Dr. Cole pronounced it a case of double pneumonia, but felt that the great naturalist was in condition to be moved. Wednesday night he was taken aboard a train and sent here, arriving shortly after midnight, where an ambulance met him and took him to the California Hospital. His condition seemed improved early yesterday morning, but at 10 o'clock it grew worse and twenty minutes later he was dead.

The body was removed to the Brown mortuary chapel and will be taken to the Muir ranch in Contra Costa county near Martinez today and the funeral will probably be held on Sunday. Mr. and Mrs. Funk will accompany the body north. Another daughter, Mrs. T. R. Hanna, lives on a ranch adjoining that owned by her late father. He was married in 1880 to Louise Strentzel, who died ten years ago.

REMARKABLE MAN

John Muir was one of the most remarkable characters of all the remarkable men and women produced by contact with the primitive West. He was born in Scotland, April 28 [sic], 1838, and came to the United States when 11 years old. For eleven years he helped his father clear a farm near Fox River, Wisc., and during that time earned enough money to go to college. He entered the University of Wisconsin at an age when the average student is finishing his course, and in 1864 he was graduated.

Mr. Muir was a man of peace. The call of nature took him to the unexplored regions of North America, where he obtained a practical experience that made him one of the greatest geologists and botanists of his time. While California was a struggling mining State, with prospects of never being much of anything else, John Muir was exploring the Yosemite Valley. He launched a campaign that conserved the natural wonders of the Yosemite and Sequoia parks by having them made national monuments.

He knew every landmark along the whole length of the Sierras, and from his lonely residence in the wilds he carried on research of animal life and vegetation. In later years the wonderful redwood forest overlooking San Francisco from an elevation across the bay, became known as the Muir Woods.

In 1879 John Muir went to Alaska and there discovered Glacier Bay. The Muir glacier, made famous by a painting by the late H. L. A. Culmer, was named for him.

A year later he led a relief expedition into the Arctic in search of the ill-fated DeLong party.

The great conservation movement which resulted in the establishment of national parks won its success through the personal efforts of John Muir. He wrote a book on "The Mountains of California" and another on "Our National Parks" as well as several volumes on nature work, study and research. His contributions to magazines and his papers read before scientific bodies brimmed with information that no other naturalist possessed.

ABLE WORKMAN

John Muir was painstaking in the production of his literary works and never produced a volume or story unless it was polished to a fine degree. He worked slowly, arduously and with tremendous success. He died with more knowledge and experience untold than he could have produced in another lifetime.

In later years the naturalist visited other parts of the world where he studied tree and plant life. He went into the jungles far up the Amazon, found the precious Baobab tree in South Africa, searched the vegetation of every continent for rare and peculiar growths, visited all the countries of the world that would interest a man of his kind and when he came home he said:

"I had a wonderful opportunity to study the three rare trees and plants I went in search of and saw many beautiful and strange things, but when it comes right down to beautiful and grand scenery, California leads the world."

MEMORIAL SERVICE

The Christmas jollification of the members of Muir Lodge of the southern branch of the Sierra Club, scheduled for Saturday night in Santa Anita Canyon, has been changed to a memorial service in honor of the noted naturalist. The mountain lovers will meet as planned, but the jollification features around the large Christmas tree will be called off. Muir Lodge was dedicated in November, 1913, in honor of Mr. Muir, the president of the Sierra Club.

Also from the *Los Angeles Times*, December 25, 1914

JOHN MUIR'S WORK

SOME NOTABLE ACHIEVEMENTS

[by A. P. Night Wire]

San Francisco, Dec. 24—John Muir, like John Burroughs, with whom his name often has been linked, belonged to that tradition of British naturalists whose work was so fused with the writer's personality and so penetrated by individual feeling that their output was as much literature as science.

Philosopher and artist, as well as observer, he took a creative delight in his work which no mere classification of details could have brought.

His descriptions of the Yosemite Valley first brought it into national fame, and his visit there left him with a love of the West which remained through all his travels and led him to make his home at Martinez in his later years. He chose a site in the Contra Costa Valley sheltered on one side by a wooded hill and surrounded on three others by vineyards, orchards and streams, confronted by the towering outline of Mt. Diablo. Within, the furnishings were in massive simplicity. Without was a riot of pines, palms, cacti and exotic vegetation, for botany, too, was one of John Muir's delights.

"But this isn't my home," he once said. "My home is in the mountains and the wilds. I am here merely for the rest my body demands. I am getting old and what once was exercise is now fatiguing exertion."

With this deep love of nature part of his very being it was fitting that John Muir should be almost as well known for his labors in behalf of forest preservation and the establishment of national reserves and parks as by his writings.

His travels, partly in company with John Burroughs, took him to Honolulu, Russia, Siberia, Manchuria, India and Australasia, but his life work was in the mountains of Western America, where he made an elaborate classification of faunal and floral life, supplemented by much descriptive writing, both in book form and in the periodical press and the newspapers. As his work became more and more widely known, Harvard, Yale, Wisconsin and other universities granted him honorary degrees and hewas elected to membership in many scientific societies. Of recent years his signature was more rarely seen, but he had remained sturdy and active until his sudden seizure by pneumonia.

The famous Muir redwood grove in Marin county, at the foot of Mt. Tamalpais, was named for the distinguished naturalist.

In the Yosemite

John Muir's exploration of the Yosemite Valley was made in winter. With a companion, the naturalist plunged into the canyon on snow-shoes, and the trip proved extremely perilous.

His sturdy build and splendid health enabled Muir to perform "hikes" through the mountains that few athletes would have been able to accomplish. On those tours through the wilds of the high Sierra, he traveled exceedingly light. On some trips, lasting weeks, his only provisions would be tea, a few cakes of chocolate and a knapsack filled with bread crumbs.

Muir had a great love of the Yosemite and his was a familiar face to summer tourists there. He was a warm advocate of a movement to make the valley accessible to visitors who came to see the Yosemite's grandeur, but he had no regard whatever for those who came to fish in the valley. He could not understand how any one could, even for the moment, neglect nature's wonders for angling. He would refer to them as being "sillier than the silly fish themselves."

INVENTIVE MIND

Muir as a lad on the farm had an inventive bent which might have rivaled that of Thomas A. Edison, had it not been discouraged by a stern parent. Among his achievements was an alarm clock device which dumped him out of bed at any desired time. This saved him the trouble of making up his mind to get up in a cold room, but he improved upon it by another clockwork system, which lighted the fire in the kitchen stove at any desired time and made it unnecessary to get up at all, for that purpose.

These and many other devices which he brought into use about the farm were disapproved by his father, who cited biblical passages against them.

Also from the *Los Angeles Times*, December 25, 1914

SEER OF GREAT WOODS
PRECIOUS INSPIRATION
by Hector Alijot

For all nature lovers Thoreau and Muir reflect the sweeter and more romantic phase of the great woods' mysteries.

While the field of the former was circumscribed by New England meadows and clearings, and the simple life of the recluse observer, the world's most rugged mountains were the stamping ground of John Muir.

It has been deplored for years that more of the wealth of material he had gathered during his long and active life was not prepared by him that naturalists might have the precious inspiration of his vision as he climbed the mountains of Manchuria, Alaska or California.

Muir acquired training in letters late in life, as he often said, owing to retarded influences independent of his own volition. He was already of age when he entered the University of Wisconsin, and this may have been the cause of his painstaking and deliberate method of writing. This in turn may explain why he did not greatly add to the large number of books we have from him. His famous "Childhood and Youth," practically his own autobiography, casts a new and fascinating light on that phase of the great man's work.

With Joseph Le Conte gone and the passing away of John Muir, California mourns the loss of its two greatest naturalists.

For those who have worshiped at the feet of John Muir, the seer of the great woods, his wonderful voice, so perfectly harmonizing with the murmurs of nature, will be heard no longer.

Somewhere in the redwoods he loved so well, on the slopes of the Sierras he knew so intimately, the figure of the inspired prophet of nature should be placed, in memory of his priceless services to the gospel of outdoors. Unfortunately, neither bronze nor marble can ever translate the magic light of the great Celt's beautiful eyes, his gentle yet convincing ways. His delightful books only remain as an imperfect mirror of the sunshine of his noble soul.

December 24, 1914

SUMMONS TO JOHN MUIR

———

Death Call Comes Suddenly for Aged Naturalist at Los Angeles

———

Was Well Known in Crown City

———

Mountains North of Pasadena Were Favorite Haunt of Beloved Man

———

John Muir, famous California naturalist and author, died at Los Angeles today of pneumonia.

The aged naturalist went to Daggett, San Bernardino county, from his home at Martinez several days ago for a visit at the home of his daughter, Mrs. J. Buell Funk. Four days ago he became ill of pneumonia. He was brought to Los Angeles quietly last night and taken to the California hospital, where he died about noon today.

Pasadena is especially interested in the work of Mr. Muir, since the mountains north of the city were among his favorite haunts. In 1877 he came to Pasadena to visit his old classmate at the Wisconsin State university, Dr. E. H. Conger, and spent much time exploring the mountains. Dr. [Hiram] Reid in his history [*History of Pasadena*, 1895], says of this trip:

"At that time no man had ever gone from Pasadena directly to the top of the mountains; Mr. Muir made the venture alone. Mrs. Conger baked three loaves of bread for him and gave him half a pound of tea, which he usually steeped by putting a little into a bottle of cold water and laying the bottle on a rock in the warm sunshine. He carried no firearms as he had conscientious scruples against taking animal life, and hence used no meat food. With provisions and blankets on his shoulder, he started and was gone three days. He made his trip to the mountains by way of Eaton's canyon; and in an article on 'The Bee Pastures of California,' published in the Century magazine for July, 1882, he gives some account of this mountain climb. It is the first account of any trip or exploration from Pasadena to our immediate mountain summits."

The trip was very hard, and he told the Congers on his return that it was one of the most difficult trips he had ever made on account of the underbrush.

Muir peak, the summit of the sloping ridge which forms the east wall of Rubio canyon and the west wall of pine canyon, is named for John Muir, the first white man to set foot on its summit.

LIFE OF NATURALIST

John Muir, geologist, explorer and naturalist, was born in Dunbar, Scotland, April 21, 1838, the son of Daniel and Anne Muir. He received his education in Scotland and at the University of Wisconsin, at the time when Dr. Ezra S. Carr of

Pasadena was a member of the faculty of the university. He married Louise Strentzel in 1880. He discovered the Muir glacier, Alaska, visited the Arctic regions on the United States steamer Corwin in search of the De Long expedition, and spent many years in work for the preservation of forests and parks. He was a member of the American Academy of Arts and Letters; fellow of the A.A.A.S.; member of the Washington Academy of Sciences, president of the Sierra Club, and member of the American Alpine Club. He was author of the following books: "The Mountains of California," in which the mountains north of Pasadena are minutely described; "Our National Parks," "Stickeen, the Story of a Dog," "My First Summer in the Sierras," "The Yosemite," [and] "Story of my Boyhood and Youth."

From his pen also came a large number of magazine and newspaper articles on the physiography and natural history of the Pacific coast and Alaska. He was editor of "Picturesque California," and in his work he traveled and studied in Russia, Siberia, Manchuria, India, Australia, New Zealand, South America and Africa.

STODDARD

Eaton Canyon

Places to Visit

Our knowledge of history is enhanced by some forays out "in the field." Several places associated with John Muir in Southern California are well worth a visit today. Exploring them will bring us closer to Muir, his Southland friends, and the landscape which endures despite a century or more of urban growth.

Access to these places may change from year to year. It would be wise to check first for their current phone numbers, hours, directions, and activities. Some of the landmarks have websites or will be developing them. The Chamber of Commerce in a town, or the Public Library, will be a good starting point to call for the status of a historic site and its current phone number.

If any of these sites are in jeopardy of being closed or left behind by history, admirers of Muir might wish to volunteer time or support, helping to keep them open for future generations.

✧ PASADENA ✧

Eaton Canyon County Park and Nature Center

1750 N. Altadena Drive, just north of New York Drive.

A beautiful Craftsman-style building, replacing the one lost in a 1993 fire, houses exhibits, classrooms, live creatures, and a large relief map showing the canyon and foothills where

John Muir first entered the San Gabriel range. Volunteer docents are skilled naturalists and welcome school groups and the public to nature walks. Outside is a natural area of 190 acres, with miles of footpaths to explore into meadows, chaparral, oak and sycamore groves, and the winter-running stream. At the head of the canyon, you can visit Eaton Canyon Falls, described by Muir as "a little poem of wildness."

Or hike from there up the Mt. Wilson Toll Road to Henninger Flat, the site of Theodore P. Lukens' forest nursery (about 5 miles round trip).

Conger and Carr home sites (including Carmelita).

The intersection of Colorado Blvd. and Orange Grove Blvd.

This busy crossroads should be visited on foot, as traffic prevents a leisurely look.

The Conger home place was at the south east corner, a sizeable acreage with house and orange groves (the land is now occupied by a parking lot and the Lodge of the Benevolent Protective Order of Elks). On New Years Day this corner holds the main reviewing stand for the Rose Parade.

The Carrs' home and gardens, called Carmelita, were on the north east corner, on land now holding the Norton Simon Museum. Both these friends of Muir chose property at the original founding point of Pasadena, high ground with the pleasantly wild Arroyo Seco to the west, sweeping views of valley and orchards to the east, and the mountain backdrop to the north.

✧ Los Angeles ✧

Lummis Home (El Alisal)

200 East Avenue 43, in the Highland Park area
   just off the 110 Freeway.

This one-of-a-kind stone home, largely built by Lummis himself, still holds a lively sense of his presence. It was the scene of his "noises": festive gatherings of artists, friends, and activists for his many causes. Muir signed into the guest book for several of these events. Today, as headquarters for the Historical Society of Southern California, the building and its native plant gardens once again come alive with history-minded celebrations and readings.

The site is open to visitors, and the Society welcomes new members to its many activities. Call them for further information.

✧ The Mountains ✧

Chantry Flat, San Gabriel Mountains

Above Arcadia, Santa Anita Avenue becomes the
   mountain road to Chantry Flat as you drive north,
   6 miles above the 210 Freeway.

This historic glen and picnic area is a starting point for hiking into the front range of the San Gabriels. A walk from here up Big Santa Anita Canyon to Sturtevant Falls (3 miles round trip) will pass the site of Muir Lodge, the Sierra Club's stone cabin destroyed by floods in 1938. Nothing remains of it to see today, but the waterfall makes a beautiful companion to your visit to Eaton Canyon Falls.

The road to Chantry Flat is sometimes closed by weather or road conditions, and parking is limited at best. But the place holds an incomparable blend of history and landscape. Consult the U.S. Forest Service office for current conditions and access information.

Chilao Visitors Center, San Gabriel Mountains

Above La Canada, take the Angeles Crest Highway (Highway 2) 27 miles north from the 210 Freeway.

At about 5200 feet elevation, this building with its exhibits and relief maps is a mecca of information about the mountain high country. Its surroundings are open forests and scattered clearings, with fragrant Jeffrey pines and a deep blue sky. The Visitors Center is closed in winter, blanketed by snow, and its re-opening is always uncertain, depending on how it has weathered the winter storms. Consult the U.S. Forest Service before driving up to see it. However, even if the building is closed, the area offers delightful rambles and picnic sites. You will be above the chaparral Muir found so dense and "shaggy", free to saunter in these high woodlands he also enjoyed.

Daggett

> 130 miles east of Los Angeles, about 10 miles east
> of Barstow on Highway I-40.

This little town, population about 200, is a walkable high desert community with several historic buildings from its mining days.   Nearby is the Mojave River, sometimes running above ground, most often underground.   The Chamber of Commerce offers a map and leaflet on historic points of interest   All around are the wide open spaces and fresh dry air (4 inches average rainfall a year) that Muir sought for his daughter Helen.

The small Daggett Museum holds local lore and memorabilia of the Muirs' time there.   Consult the town's Chamber of Commerce to determine when the museum is open.

Indian Canyons, near Palm Springs

> 4 miles south of downtown Palm Springs, taking
> Palm Canyon Drive south

 This preserve consists of three canyons: Murray, Palm, and Andreas, now in the care of the Agua Caliente Band of Cahuilla Indians. Jeep and walking tours are often available, or you may hike on your own. These are the picturesque scenes where the Muir and Lukens families so enjoyed their camping and the desert dawns. The canyons are best visited in the cooler seasons—although Muir and his party seemed to relish the summer heat. Not far away is Tahquitz Canyon, also visited on that Muir-Lukens outing of 1905.

Call the Indian Canyons Preserve for further information.

About the Author

Photo by Hortensia Chu

Elizabeth Pomeroy holds a Ph.D. in English from UCLA. She is an active Sierra Club member and teaches English at Pasadena City College. She has written articles on literature and history, and her recent books include *Reading the Portraits of Queen Elizabeth I* and *Lost and Found: Historic and Natural Landmarks of the San Gabriel Valley*, a selection from her regular newspaper columns on historic places.

About the Artists

Joseph Stoddard is an artist who lives and works in Pasadena. He has produced many images for books, posters and magazines about the Southland and never goes anywhere without his sketch book and miniature paint box. A selection of his watercolors was recently published in the book *Pasadena Sketchbook*.

Hortensia Chu is a graphic designer and illustrator who also resides in Pasadena. She has designed many book covers and collaborated with Joseph Stoddard on other Southern California publications. She has been the art director for the projects of Many Moons Press.